ISBN 978-1-331-33893-2
PIBN 10176383

THE MONARCHY ACCORDING TO THE CHARTER.

BY THE

VISCOUNT DE CHATEAUBRIAND,

PEER OF FRANCE, MINISTER OF STATE, CHEVALIER OF THE ROYAL AND MILITARY ORDER OF ST. LOUIS, MEMBER OF THE ROYAL INSTITUTE OF FRANCE.

"THE KING, THE CHARTER, AND HONEST MEN."

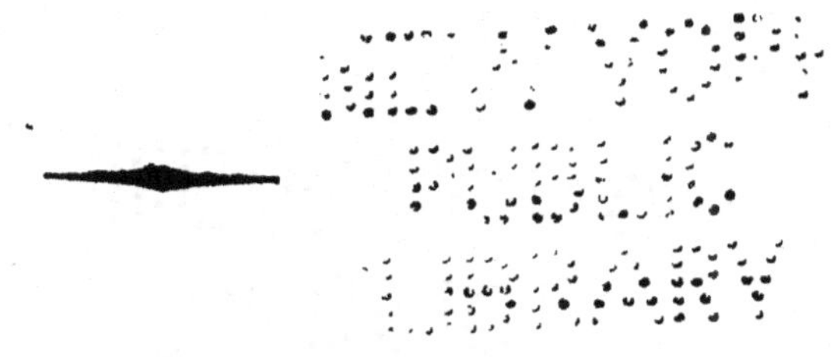

LONDON:

PRINTED FOR JOHN MURRAY, ALBEMARLE-STREET.

1816.

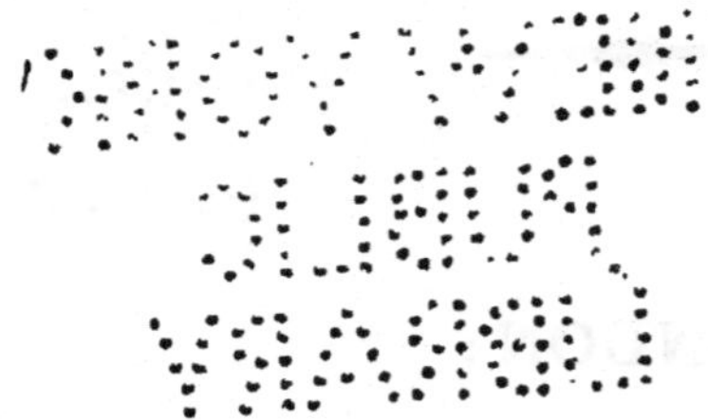

PREFACE.

IF, when only a private citizen, I considered myself bound, on certain important occasions, to address my country, what ought I not *now* to do? As a Peer and Minister of France, have I not higher duties to perform, and should not my efforts for my King be in proportion to the honours which he has bestowed on me?

As a Peer of France, it is my duty to declare the truth to France, and I will declare it.

As a Minister, it is my duty to declare the truth to the King, and I will declare it.

If the Council, of which I have the honour to be a Member, was ever assembled, I might be told—"Give your advice in Council;" but that Council does not meet. I am therefore obliged to resort to other means to make my humble remonstrances, and to fulfil the first duty of a Minister.

Need I prove by examples that men in place have the right of discussing in this form matters of State? Examples are abundant; I should find several in France, and England furnishes a long series. From Bolingbroke to Burke, I could cite a great number of Lords, of Members of the House of Commons, and Members of the Privy Council, who have written on politics, and in direct opposition to the Minister of the day.

And shall it be said, that, if France appear to me to be menaced with new misfortunes; if the legitimate Monarchy is in danger, I must be silent because I am a Privy Councellor and Peer! On the contrary, it is my duty to point out the danger, to fire the signal of distress, and to call for help. For this reason I have, for the first time in my life, affixed my titles to my name, in order to announce my duties, and to add, if I can, to this work, the weight of my political rank.

These duties are the more imperious, since individual liberty and the liberty of the press are suspended. Who dares—who *can* speak?

Since the title of Peer of France gives me, by virtue of the Charter, a sort of inviolability, it is my duty to make use of it in order to restore to Public Opinion a portion of its power. The Public Opinion says · "You have made laws which shackle us; speak, then, for us, since you have deprived us of utterance"

Finally, the public has sometimes lent me a favourable ear: I have some chance of being heard. If, then, by writing I can hope to do good, be it ever so little, my conscience commands me to go on.

This Preface should terminate here, had I not some explanations to make.

The word *royalist*, in this work, is taken in a very extended sense: it embraces all royalists, whatever may be the shades of their opinions, provided their opinions be not dictated by the *moral* interests* of the revolution.

By *Representative Government*, I understand Monarchy, such as it at present exists in France,

* What I understand by revolutionary *moral interests*, will be seen in the course of this work. See Chapter 59.

in England, and in the Netherlands, whether the strict accuracy of the expression be admitted or not.

When I speak of the faults, the systems, or the *ordonnances*, of an Administration, I do not implicate personally the Ministers who composed, or who may now compose such Administration. Consequently I have not spared even those Administrations in which I had friends. I feel, for instance, a particular respect for the Chancellor of France. I have frequently had occasion to recognize in him that candour, that integrity of mind and heart, and that high probity which distinguished our ancient Magistracy. My sentiments for the Count de Blacas are well known. I have stated them in my writings, and in my speeches in the Chamber of Peers. The King has not a more honest, a more generous, nor a more devoted servant, than M. de Blacas. He displays, even at this moment, his ability by the manner in which he conducts the difficult negociations with which he is entrusted. Would to God that he could have exercised a greater influence over the

Ministry of which he formed a part! But in fact that Ministry committed enormous faults, and I have pronounced a rigorous judgment upon them, without implicating either the Chancellor or M. de Blacas, who, far from participating in the system of the Administration, constantly opposed them. In a work, however, in which I discuss the principles of *Representative Monarchy*, I was bound to admit the principle that *a ministerial measure is the work of the whole administration.*

CONTENTS.

THE MONARCHY

ACCORDING TO

THE CHARTER.

CHAPTER I.

INTRODUCTION.

FRANCE desires her legitimate king.

There are three modes of government which might exist under the legitimate king.

1. The old regime.
2. A despotism.
3. The charter.

The old regime is now impossible—as I have shewn elsewhere*

Despotism could only be established by having—like Buonaparte, six hundred thousand

* The present work being, as it were, a continuation of my *Reflexions Politiques*, I shall, whenever I fall upon the same topics, quote the *Reflexions*, to avoid repetitions; for the same reason, I shall quote the "*Rapport fait au Roi à Gand*," a paper founded on the principles I had endeavoured to establish in the "*Reflexions Politiques*."

soldiers devoted to their leader—an iron hand —an audacious spirit: nothing of this exists.

I have seen too well how a despotism may be established; but I cannot conceive how a Bourbon can become a despot.

There remains then the legitimate monarchy under the constitutional charter.

This is the only good mode now left to us: besides, it is the only *possible*. *That* decides the question.

CHAPTER II.

INTRODUCTION CONTINUED.

We start then with this fact—WE HAVE A CHARTER, AND WE CAN HAVE NOTHING BUT THIS CHARTER.

But it is truly wonderful to see how, living under it, we have contrived to mistake the spirit and character of the charter.

Why is it so?—Because, carried away by our passions, our interests, our temper, we have, while professing to adopt its principles, always endeavoured to escape from the results to which these principles lead;—because we are mad enough to hope to render coexistent, things contradictory and impossible;—because, instead of following the natural course of the established government, we oppose its spirit and thwart its operation—because, perplexed by the novelties of our situation, we have not the courage to brave slight inconveniences for the sake of great and permanent advantages—because, after having made *liberty* the foundation of our institutions, we are afraid of it, and are inclined to take refuge in the tranquillity of arbitrary power; not being able to understand how a government can be vigorous without being despotic.

I shall endeavour to state some plain and useful truths on the subject of the practical exercise of a representative monarchy.

I shall begin with *principles.* I shall endeavour to show what we possess; what we must add; what we ought to retrench—what is reasonable, what is absurd.

I shall next observe upon our *systems.* I shall detail those which have hitherto succeeded each other. I shall mark what I consider their faults, and I shall propose what I conceive to be the remedy.

In discoursing of *principles* and *systems*, I hope to adhere, above all, to the plain principles of *common sense*, a rarer quality than its name indicates—alas! the Revolution has so confounded all our ideas, that in politics, as well as religion, France has to begin again with the catechism.

CHAPTER III.

THE ELEMENTS OF A REPRESENTATIVE MONARCHY.

WHAT is a representative government?—its origin?—how has it grown up in Europe?—how did it formerly exist in France and England?—how was it lost by our ancestors?—why has it survived among our neighbours?—By what steps, finally, have we returned to this system? For all these questions I must refer to *Les Reflexions Politiques*.

But this, at least, is clear: the government established by the charter is composed of four elements—the King, or the Royal prerogative; the House of Peers; the House of Deputies; the Ministry.

This machine, less complicated than the organization of the ancient monarchy before Louis XIV, is, on that very account, more delicate, and requires a nicer touch. Violence would break it, want of skill stop it.

Let us examine what is wanting in this new machine, and what hitches we have hitherto found in its operation.

CHAPTER IV.

OF THE ROYAL PREROGATIVE, AND ITS FUNDAMENTAL PRINCIPLE.

THE doctrine of a constitutional royal prerogative is—that nothing is done directly by the King himself; that every act of government is in truth his Ministers', though the thing be done in his Majesty's name, or the document signed by his Majesty's hand.

Laws proposed —* *ordonnances* — choice of men and of measures—for all these, Ministers alone are responsible.

The King of a representative monarchy is, as it were, a divinity, placed beyond our reach, inviolable and infallible. His person is sacred, and his will can do no wrong. If there be error, it is the error of his servants.

We may therefore discuss public affairs without offence to the Monarch, and we may criticise measures which, though in his name, are the mere acts of his Ministers.

* I have not attempted to translate this word, which is sufficiently intelligible, but for which we have no adequate English term; it most resembles our *order in council*.—Tr.

CHAPTER V.

APPLICATION OF THIS PRINCIPLE.

When the conduct of Ministers alarms a loyal nation; when the name of the King is employed to give effect to faults or follies; then Ministers either abuse our credulity, or are themselves in a deplorable ignorance of the first principles of a representative government.

The most devoted Royalist in either house may therefore venture to push aside this shield, though blasoned with the King's image, and attack the Minister who stands behind it. Our business is with him—not with the King.

And all this is founded in reason.

For when a King is surrounded with responsible advisers—while he is himself above or beyond all responsibility—it is clear that he must permit them to act according to their own views; because it is to their account alone that events are to be charged, either in praise or censure. If they were the mere executors of the royal will, they could not, with any pretence of justice, be attacked for measures not their own.

But it will be asked, "what, then, is the duty of the King in the administration?"

If the Minister adopts or follows the suggestions which his Majesty may make in council, he is certain of acting rightly, and he will have the universal concurrence of the nation; but if he overrules or neglects the royal opinion, he increases his own responsibility, but the King's exists no longer. The Minister goes on, executes his own design,—fails,—falls,—and the King chooses a wiser successor.

But even if the King should accept erroneous advice of his Minister, and the measure fail, the King is still unanswerable for the failure. Ministers have a thousand opportunities of deceiving and convincing a King, even contrary to his better judgment. He is obliged to take the case as they state it; and corruption, passion, incapacity, have each a thousand colours in which they may present their object to the royal eye.

In fact, nothing is the King's but the law—which he sanctions—the happiness of his people—and the prosperity of his country.

I have the rather insisted on this doctrine, because it has been misunderstood. The devotion of the Chamber of Deputies to his Majesty's sacred person has been abused: the members of that admirable assembly hesitated to oppose any thing which was produced to them in the King's name, and they hardly knew how to act when, in the name of the King, they were invited to attack the best interests of the throne.

Let us now proceed from this general principle to the details.

CHAPTER VI.

CONTINUATION OF THE ROYAL PREROGATIVE. —THE KING'S INITIATIVE.—ORDONNANCES.

THE Royal prerogative ought to be stronger in France than in England *.

But, sooner or later, it must be relieved from an embarrassment which arises from the Charter itself. By giving *exclusively* to the King the initiation of laws, it was intended to strengthen the prerogative, and the effect has been to weaken it.

The *form* in which this power is exercised is as inconvenient as the *principle* is false: Ministers come down to the Houses with their proposed law in the shape of an *ordonnance* —" *Louis, by the grace of God,*" &c. The Ministers thus borrow the individual person and identity of his Majesty; they make him propose this law as the result of his own wisdom and meditation; then the law is discussed; then come alterations, omissions, and amendments; and the wisdom of the King receives a legislative denial in the rejection of his first conceptions. Then must come a second *or-*

* See *Reflexions Politiques.*

donnance to declare (still by the grace of God, and the wisdom of the King), that the wisdom of the King had been deceived, and that the grace of God had been invoked in vain.

All this is miserable, and injurious to the royal person and royal dignity. It must be changed; and this solemn form must be reserved for the final sanction of the law—the peculiar duty of the Crown when the legislature shall have done theirs—and not for the sketch of a law proposed by Ministers, and liable to alteration, and even rejection, by the legislature.

On all occasions these Royal *ordonnances* should be used with moderation. The style and form they assume is that of *absolute* authority, because the King of France was *formerly* the supreme legislator; but NOW that his legislative functions are divided with the two houses, it is more decent, it is more legal, it is more constitutional, that the Crown should speak with absolute authority, *only* when it ratifies and perfects the law, which the wisdom of the other branches of the legislature has previously framed.

Else, the peer and the deputy will be placed between two distinct legislative powers—between the old and the new constitution—between the duty they owe to the *ordonnance* as subjects, and the duty they owe to their constituents as legislators. How can they freely and honestly debate such an ordonnance without disrespect to the Royal prerogative? How can they refrain from debating it, without an abandonment of principle?

The present practice would at length lead to one or other of the following serious inconveniences—either the King's name would produce a degree of respect inconsistent with free discussion—or a free discussion would soon impair the respect due to the King's name, and tend to a degradation of the Royal authority—in which, and in which alone, consist our hopes of tranquillity and happiness.

Every one knows, that, in England, the wise rules of parliament and the constitution would be infringed by a member's using the name of the King, either in support of, or in opposition to, any proposition whatsoever.

CHAPTER VII.

OBJECTION.

" But if the Chambers have alone the initiative, or if they enjoy that right in common with the Crown, shall we not revive that mania of law-making which has once before, under the constituent assembly, overturned the constitution, and desolated the country?"

This objection forgets that the spirit of the nation was not *then*, what it is *now*; that the revolution was then beginning, that it is now ended; that the minds of men are now tending to repose, as then to motion; and that instead of a spirit of pulling down, the general wish is now to repair and strengthen.

—The objection forgets, too, that the constitutions are not the same—there was then but one assembly, or two councils of the same nature. Now the Charter has established two distinct Chambers, composed of very different elements; these Chambers are a mutual check, and one of them would serve to restrain, when necessary, any rash impetuosity of the other.

—The objection too forgets that motions can be no longer made in the heat of the moment, and debated on the instant and in a hurry—that every proposition must be stated in writing, and laid on the table—that if the Chambers decide that it is fit to entertain the proposition, it cannot be discussed but after an interval of three days—that it is then referred to the Committees—and that it is not till after these processes, that it returns to the Chambers modified, and, as it were, *cooled*, to be examined—to be debated—to be amended—perhaps to be still longer retarded, if there happen to be other orders of the day which have a priority.—And, finally, it forgets that the King has the power—the absolute power—of rejecting the law, and of dissolving the Chambers if the public interest should require this measure.

Besides, what is it we propose? "To abolish the Royal initiative?"—by no means. Leave the initiative to the Crown, which will employ it on great and popular occasions; but give it *also* to the Chambers, which in fact possess it already, since they have by the Charter the right of suggesting laws.

"But," it is answered, "the suggestion of a law must be in a secret sitting; with the initiative the discussion would be public. Deliberative assemblies have done so much mischief to France that we cannot too carefully guard ourselves against them."

But why then, if this be true, why have a charter? why a free constitution? why not have taken things as they were—a passive senate, a mute legislature?

And thus it is, by a fatal inconsistency, that in the same breath we invoke and disparage the charter, we would and we would not.

Do you know what will happen if you are not more decided in your views and wishes—more consistent with yourselves? Either you will destroy the Constitution—and God knows what the result of that would be—or you will be carried off by it. Take care, for, in the present state of things, it is probably stronger than you are.

CHAPTER VIII.

AGAINST THE SECRET SUGGESTION OF LAWS.

THE *secret* suggestion of *laws!*—The very idea is false and contradictory; it is an absurdity of which we must get rid. This secret suggestion can never be *so* secret that it will not transpire; and then it will come before the public disfigured and falsified.

The free and open proposition of laws is the essence of a representative Government. In such a Government all should be known, all should be open to public observation. If the debates should become violent, five members concurring can, under the 44th article of the Charter, cause the galleries to be cleared.

Thus the advantages of secrecy would be combined with those of publicity; and there is therefore nothing gained by denying the Chambers the public initiative. It is only doing in one way what you might better and more simply do in another; it is complicating the springs of a machine to produce an effect which it naturally would have had without any additional effort.

The conceding the initiative to the Chambers

would remove all those refinements upon abstract principles which have this last year embarrassed the discussions of every law that has been proposed; we should hear no more the eternal and complicated disputes about *amendments*. Common sense requires that the Chambers, who are employed in the framing of a law, should have the right of proposing whatever amendments they shall think necessary to its perfection (with the exception of the budget, however, as I shall presently state); to endeavour to assign precise limits to the proposal of amendments, to determine the shade at which an amendment ends and a proposition begins; to decide at what point it is that the amendment trenches upon the prerogative: all this is a wide waste of political metaphysics, in which we lose our time and bewilder our understandings.

Let the Government—(not, however, by an *ordonnance*, *By the grace of God*,)—and let each member of the Chambers, have the right of proposing laws, and all these cobweb discussions are swept away at once. Instead then of perpetually calling one another to order,—instead of declaiming against fancied violations of the Charter,—instead of affected anxieties for the Royal prerogative,—instead of rejecting an amendment, not because it is wrong, but because it contradicts some unintelligible theory;—instead of all this tissue of perplexity and nonsense, we shall be obliged to discuss the subject on the grounds of public utility, and in its general operation. We shall be able to look at the whole matter in one view, and we shall have done with mutual accusations, of democratic principles on one hand, and of passive obedience on the other. Our judgments will be enlightened, our tempers will be moderated, and at least—there will be a world of time and trouble saved.

CHAPTER IX.

THE CONSEQUENCES OF GRANTING THE INITIATIVE TO THE CHAMBERS.

To grant the initiative to the Chambers is clearly the interest of the King—the Crown would then propose only acts of grace and popularity, and would leave all the more painful duties of legislation to the Peers and Deputies.

Then if a law should be rejected, the name of the King will at least have been respected, and the Royal dignity spared the applause or the censure of the galleries—then we should no longer have Ministers working upon the conscience of the loyal, by exclaiming, "It is the "King's proposal—it is his royal will—his Ma"jesty never can consent to this or that amend"ment."

If Ministers are fit for their high stations, the initiative thus granted to the Chambers will be, in fact, no other than the initiative of the Government itself; it is no great compliment to say that such men could procure the proposal of any reasonable measure.

When an author publishes a work anonymously, he has an alternative advantage:—if the work fails he is silent and safe; if it succeeds he claims all the honour, and the profit—Ministers would be even better off than authors—for, good or bad, the measures which their friends should thus propose, would probably have the support of a majority of the members.

Unless, indeed, the system so ingeniously invented amongst us in the last session, of carrying every point by the minority, should be permanently adopted;—when we abandon the plain common sense of carrying measures only by a majority, we attempt to walk without feet, to fly without wings—we break the main-spring of representative Government.

I shall return to this subject by and by.

CHAPTER X.

THE FOREGOING OBSERVATIONS ENFORCED.

I HAVE stated the *inconvenience* of the right of secret proposition or rather *suggestion* now vested in the Chambers, and of the public initiative by the Crown. I shall now trace some of its *absurdities*.

If the *suggestion* should pass the two Chambers, it goes to the Crown ; if the Crown adopts it, it comes back to the Chambers, in the form of the project of a law.

If the Chambers should, after all this, choose to make an amendment, the proposition must go back to the King, who may in his turn insert other amendments, which must then return to the Chambers to be adopted by them, and sent back again to the King, who may again exercise his right of alteration—and so on.

In the province of Kiang-nan, one of the most civilised in China, when two Mandarins have any business to do, he who has received the first visit testifies his politeness by accompanying the visitor back to his own door ; the visitor of course is equally polite, and sees his neighbour home to his house—the latter, however, is too well bred to remain in debt to his friend in a point of civility, and therefore insists on conducting him back in great form; the other is equally polite and ceremonious, and so on, backwards and forwards, till—at last it sometimes happens that,—in this laborious interchange of peripatetic politeness, the too-well bred Mandarins expire,—and the business with them.*

* Lettres édifiantes.

CHAPTER XI.

CONTINUATION OF THE SAME SUBJECT.

THE *initiative* and the final *sanction* of a law are manifestly incompatible; for in this case the Crown approves or disapproves its own work.

Besides the absurdity of the thing, the Crown is thus placed in a situation beneath its dignity. It cannot approve the result of its own wisdom and labour, till a majority of the Chambers have criticised and approved it. Can it be doubted that it is more reasonable, more decent, more dignified, that the Chambers should discuss and propose, and that the King should examine and approve? Then the King would appear in his proper character, the supreme and final legislator. "It is good,—it is bad. I approve,—I disapprove." Such should be HIS share in the law: every one would be then in his proper place, and humble individuals would be no longer obliged by law, to criticise or reject measures proposed by the wisdom and the patriotism of the Sovereign.

I think I have shewn that this *initiative*, far

from being favourable to the Crown, is, in fact, anti-monarchical, because it displaces persons and powers. The English very sensibly commit this function to their Houses of Parliament.

. . .

. . . .

CHAPTER XII.

A DOUBT.

It will be asked, "is the King then, in a representative government, a mere idol?—an image which we adore, but which has neither motion or power?"

There is the mistake. The King, in such a monarchy, is more absolute than any monarch of France has been before him; more powerful than the Sultan at Constantinople; more *Master* at Paris, than Louis XIV. at Versailles.

He is accountable only to God and his conscience.

He is the head, or visible prelate, of the Gallican church.

He is the father of all private families, the example of their duties, and the fountain of their education and morals.

He alone rejects or sanctions laws—the law resides in him, and emanates from his person—he is, then, the sovereign legislator.

He is even above the law, for he has the attribute of mercy, and the rigour of the law is silent before him.

He appoints and dismisses his Ministers of his own mere motion—without opposition, without control: all authority flows from him.

The army obeys the orders of the King alone.

He alone makes war or peace.

He is therefore the supreme head of the civil state.

The Chief, thus, of all that constitutes a nation—its religion, morals, politics—he holds in his hand the manners, the laws, the ministry, the police, the army, and the power of peace and of war!

He drops his extended hand—the whole machine stops.

He raises it—all is again in motion.

He is so completely identified and mixed with every thing, that, take away the King, and there is nothing.

What, then, do you regret? what power, what splendor, is wanting? Is it the net of fetters with which the old Monarchy was embarrassed? Is it the power which Ministers possessed, of clapping you in the Bastille?

You are mistaken, if you believe that the Crown had formerly a more free and independent authority than it now has. What King of the ancient time could have raised the enormous revenue of the last budget? what King could have exercised so violent a power as that with which the laws relative to the liberty of the press, individual liberty*, and seditious cries, have armed the Crown?

Having said thus much on the Royal Prerogative, let us next turn to the Chamber of Peers.

* A law lately passed, similar to our suspension of the *Habeas Corpus* act.—*Trans.*

CHAPTER XIII.

OF THE CHAMBER OF PEERS: ITS NECESSARY PRIVILEGES.

If—before I had received from the munificence of the King the dignity of the peerage—I had not ventured to make for the Chamber of Peers those claims which I am now about to repeat, a personal motive of disinclination might perhaps prevent my now doing so; but my *published sentiments having preceded those honours which infinitely overpay my humble efforts in the Royal Cause, I may be permitted to treat this matter with a greater freedom.

The Chamber of Peers ought to possess—not for its individual interests, but for those of the King and the people—higher privileges, honours, and fortune.

In the Report, however, which I made to the King in Council at Ghent, in submitting the necessity of making the peerage hereditary—(for the purpose, as well of establishing the basis of the Charter, as of proving the sincerity of the promises which had been made,)—I never thought of recommending that *all* the peerages

* *Reflex. Pol.—Rapp. à Gand.*

should *all at once* be made hereditary. A certain number of peers, selected from the old and the new nobility, might have sufficed in the first instance. The Ministry, who issued the *Ordonnance* of the 19th of August, 1815, did perhaps not see how much that measure took from the Crown.

The King readily followed the natural impulse of his generosity, and gave with both hands every thing of grace and favour which he could bestow; but the Ministry who guided his hands were surely ill advised—the fountain of honour and reward is exhausted—the noble aim of a noble ambition is removed; what would not have been the public services of a peer *for life* desirous of earning for his posterity this eminent and important dignity!

That *ordonnance* would seem to deprive the King of the power of creating in future peerages for life; but it must surely be some clerical error, for the Charter, art. 27, expressly states, "the King can at his will create peers for life, or make them hereditary."

CHAPTER XIV.

ENTAILS.—THE ESSENCE OF THE PEERAGE.

I SHALL not here repeat what I have said in the *Reflexions Politiques* on the honours and privileges which should be conferred on the peerage.

I shall only add, that, sooner or later, we must re-establish the right of *entailing* property in the order of primogeniture;—transferred from the Roman law into ours, but for other purposes, entails are necessary ingredients in a system of constitutional monarchy.

The revival of the power of redeeming alienated lands (*le retrait lignager*) would also be beneficial: this process, which took its origin in the period when fiefs became hereditary, would connect the dignity with the estate, and the *titled land* would make a nobleman more certainly and satisfactorily than the will of a minister.

Stat fortuna domus et avi numerantur avorum.

Such are the means by which might be re-established in France *aristocratic families*, the barriers and safeguards of the throne:—without privilege, without property, the peerage is an empty name, an institution which does not fulfil its object.

When the Peers have inferior titles, and less territorial property, than the Deputies, the political balance is destroyed—the natural force of the aristocracy either is lost, or goes to swell the democratic importance of the Chamber of Deputies.

This Chamber—becoming, thus, both the aristocracy and democracy, both the Lords and Commons of the nation—will acquire a dangerous but inevitable preponderance, uniting to its natural and legitimate popularity, the *equality of titles and the superiority of fortune.

But when and how can these advantages be annexed to the peerage? Time must show. I only repeat, that, do what we will, we must come to that,—or Representative Monarchy will not establish itself in France.

Farther;—the sittings of the Chamber of Peers ought to be public—not perhaps by law,

* It is right to explain to our English readers that at present the French peerage confers no title—some peers are plain Mr. Such-a-thing; while in the Chamber of Deputies there are a vast number, probably a majority, of *titled* gentlemen. Formerly, under the old regime, the *Duc et Pair*, who sat in the High Court of Parliament, had a kind of relation to our *peers*; but the ordinary titles of nobility neither gave nor give any political honour. M. de Chateaubriand recommends an approximation to the English constitution in this particular.—*Trans.*

but, as in England, by custom and tolerance. Without this publicity the Chamber of Peers has not a sufficient action on the public opinion, and leaves too great an advantage in this particular to the Chamber of Deputies.

The interest of the Ministry itself would require this publicity. In the natural order of things, the attacks on ministers commence in the popular Chamber, and the defence is to be made in the House of Peers: the attack then is public, and the defence secret; two opposite rules are thus applied to one cause. Thus there is a contradiction in the law; and injustice to the party.

Let us now turn to the Chamber of Deputies.

CHAPTER XV.

OF THE CHAMBER OF DEPUTIES: ITS RELATION WITH MINISTERS.

Our Chamber of Deputies would be perfectly well constituted, if the laws for regulating elections, and those regarding the responsibility of Ministers, were conclusively framed. But the Chamber is as yet deficient in the precise knowledge of its own powers, and of those truths which can only be the children of experience.

Its first duty is to cause itself to be respected. It ought not to suffer Ministers to establish any principle of independence of the legislature, or of being at liberty to attend or not, as they may please, the summons of the Chambers. In England, Ministers are liable to be questioned not only on legislative proceedings, but on questions of their individual administration, on the appointments which they make, and even upon articles of news which appear in the public journals.

If that sweeping phrase which we have lately heard, " Ministers are accountable for their *administration** to the King only," be tolerated, we shall soon see that every thing will be *administration:* incapable Ministers may then ruin the country at their ease; and the Chamber, become their slaves, will fall into disrepute and disgrace.

"But what means have the Chambers of making themselves heard? If Ministers refuse to answer them, how can they oblige them? and will they not, by a summons which they cannot enforce, impair their dignity, and render themselves ridiculous, by an empty presumption?"

I reply that the Chamber has several modes of maintaining its rights.

Let us state the true principles of this question.

The Chambers have a right of putting to the Ministers what questions they please.

The Ministers ought always to attend, and to answer whenever the Chambers desire it.

Ministers are not indeed on all occasions bound to enter into explanations. They may decline doing so, but they should ground their refusal on reasons of state, of which in due

* The French use the word *administration* as contradistinguished from legislature, finance, or justice, to signify the mere civil duties of government, and the actual execution of these duties by the Minister and his subordinates.—*Trans.*

time the Chambers may be informed. The Chambers, treated with this attention, will go no further. A Minister demanded that six millions per annum should be placed at his disposal; he gave his word of honour that it was necessary for the public service, and the Deputies did not hesitate to vote it without any further explanation.—"Upon the honour of a gentleman" is an old pledge, on which a Frenchman will always obtain credit.

Again; the Chambers will never interfere in the administration of affairs, will never create inconvenient discussions, will never expose the Ministry to real embarrassment, *if* the Ministers are what they ought to be,—masters of the Chambers in fact, and their servants in form.

But how shall we attain this desirable result? Very easily:—the Ministry must be identified with the majority of the Chambers, and act with it,—else no government can go on.

I am aware that the kind of authority which the Chambers during their session exercise over the Ministry, recalls to our minds the usurpations of the Constituent Assembly. But, again I say, comparisons between that day and this are not only odious but lame.

I deny that the experience of that period forbids us to hope that we may establish a representative monarchy in France. That Government was not a representative Monarchy founded on natural principles, and balanced by a real distribution of powers—one absolute assembly, and a Monarch whose *veto* was not absolute! What resemblance is there between the political system under the Constituent Assembly and ours under the Charter.

Let us give the Charter a fair trial: if it fails—if the public opinion and the public service do not go on with it, *then* we may say that a representative Government is not suited to the feelings of France; but, *until then*, we have no right to condemn that which we have never tried.

CHAPTER XVI.

THE CHAMBER OF DEPUTIES SHOULD CAUSE ITSELF TO BE TREATED WITH RESPECT BY THE PUBLIC JOURNALS.

The Chamber of Deputies should not permit itself to be *collectively* insulted in the public papers, or the *speeches* of its members to be altered or disfigured.

As long as the Press shall be in bondage, the Deputies have a right to consider Ministers as responsible for its errors: because, in this case, the censors are the persons to blame, and the censors are nothing but the agents of the Ministers.

When the Press shall become free, the Deputies may call a libeller to their own bar, or may direct a public prosecution against him in the courts of justice.

Until the Press shall really be free, the Chamber might have a journal of its own, in which its own debates might be given with accuracy, and which would render indifferent the errors or malice of the other papers.

But that which is above all things necessary is *the Liberty of the Press*. Let us lose no time in claiming it—and for these reasons:—

CHAPTER XVII.

THE LIBERTY OF THE PRESS.

Without the Liberty of the Press there can be no representative Government.

A representative Government is founded on and enlightened by public opinion; the Chambers cannot be aware of that opinion if the opinion has no organ.

In a representative Government there are two tribunals—the Chambers, where the interests of the people are debated; the public, in which the conduct of the Chambers is discussed.

In the differences which may arise between the Ministers and the Chambers, how is the public to know the truth if the journals are under the restraint of the Ministers themselves, an interested party in the dispute? How shall the Ministers and the Chambers ascertain the public opinion, if the Press, *the tongue of the people*, be not free?

CHAPTER XVIII.

THE PRESS IN THE HANDS OF THE POLICE DESTROYS THE CONSTITUTIONAL BALANCE.

In a constitutional Monarchy the powers of the Monarch and of the Legislature must be consistent and balanced. But if you throw the Press into the scale of the Ministers, and permit them to employ it exclusively in their own favour, they will soon turn the public opinion against the Chambers: the balance is destroyed, and the constitution in danger.

CHAPTER XIX.

CONTINUATION OF THE SAME SUBJECT.

WHAT in fact happens when the press (by the mediation of a censor) is in the hands of Ministers ?—Their gazettes applaud all they do, all they say, all that their party does or says

—intrà muros et extrà.

Those journals the applause of which they cannot command, they at least can condemn to silence.

—I have seen anti-ministerial papers suspended for having only praised such or such an opinion.

—I have seen the speeches of Deputies mutilated by the censors, and eve *c orrected* by these obliging revisers.

—I have seen the papers especially forbidden to mention a fact or a publication* which happened to displease some Minister.

* The work I now publish will, no doubt, afford fresh instances of these kinds of abuse. The journals will be commanded either to abuse or to refuse to advertise it. If any of them should venture to mention it independently, it will be stopped at the post-office, according to custom. I shall, I dare say, see, ay, and *feel* too, the good old times of

I have seen a censor who had suffered eleven years imprisonment as a Royalist, dismissed from his employment for having permitted one of the journals to insert an article in favor of the Royalists.

At last it has been discovered that these *written* mandates from the police might involve the

Fouché and Savary. Nay, libels against me have been published under the Royal Police, which Savary himself had suppressed as too atrocious. I never complained, because I am sincerely the friend of the freedom of the press, and that according to my principles I could only complain to the laws—and there are none. Besides, I am accustomed to insults of this nature, and in truth grown somewhat callous. I individually am but one of little importance, but the principles of my work may be of some; and for this reason I would entreat the public not to judge of it from the reports of the journals. It attacks a powerful party—that party has the exclusive dominion of these journals;—literature and politics continue to be made at the old shop in the police-office—I may then expect every kind of attack; but I may also venture to beg not to be condemned till I shall have been read.

M. de Chateaubriand, with all his foresight, was not prepared for so extravagant an exercise of arbitrary power as he has suffered: two editions of his work have been actually seized as if it were treason, and his own name has been struck out of the list of Privy Counsellors, as if he was a traitor. The name of this admirable writer, great statesman, and loyal subject, who followed the King into his exile at Ghent, is erased from the list of his Majesty's Counsellors, —and by what hand?—Alas, for the poor King of France! *Trans.*

parties in some little difficulties; they have therefore been of late abandoned, and the editors have been acquainted that they would henceforward receive their instructions *verbally*. Thus the proofs of unconstitutional interference are destroyed, and the commands of the Minister may be, if necessary, explained away as the mistake of an editor.

Thus it is that France is insulted, and Europe deceived; thus it is that there is no sort of calumny which has not been heaped upon the Chambers. It is lucky that they are so flagrantly absurd and contradictory: we might have been alarmed at finding ourselves called aristocrats,—ultra-royalists,—enemies of the Chamber,—and *white* jacobins, if we had not found ourselves in the next page designated as democrats—enemies of the royal prerogative—a faction stickling for the clerical errors of the charter—and finally *black* jacobins!!!—This consoled us.

It is utterly impossible, it is contrary to all principles of a free Government, to leave the Press in the control of Ministers—to give them the power of indulging, through it, their caprices, their passions, and their interests; of disguising their crimes, and of poisoning the sources of truth.

If the Press were free, the Deputies and their

assailants would be fairly at the bar of public opinion, which would then find no difficulty in deciding on the talents of the parties, and the justice of the cause.

In the name of God, let us be at least consistent; renounce, if you will, this representative Government; but if we pretend to maintain it, let us have the Liberty of the Press. Under abuses such as I have described, no free constitution can exist.

CHAPTER XX.

DANGERS OF THE FREEDOM OF THE PRESS.—JOURNALS.—REGULATIONS.

" But the freedom of the press is not without inconvenience."

Granted—it is not without danger; and it can only be permitted to exist in the presence of a strong law, *immanis lex*, which should repress falsehood by ruin, calumny by disgrace, sedition by imprisonment or exile, and treason by death! but all this power must be in the *laws alone*. I demand for authors and editors the freedom of the press,—but at their own risk and peril: if we do not obtain it, the constitution is undone.

As to the Journals—the most dangerous weapon—the abuse might be easily restrained, by obliging the proprietors to give security. This security would afford a guarantee for any fines—the simplest and safest mode of punishment—which the tribunals might inflict.

This security should be to the amount of a capital which supposes the contribution to the state of 1000 francs (about 45*l.*), which is the amount of contribution that qualifies a member of the Chamber of Deputies.

I propose this rate, because I consider the functions of the Deputy and the Journalist to be, in one point of view, analogous;—it is the privilege and the duty of both to discuss public men and public measures, to advise the people, and to influence in some degree the measures of the state: they ought both, therefore, to be persons who have some stake in the country, who have something to gain by good order and national prosperity, and something to lose by disorder and public calamity.

We should then be relieved from the swarms of public papers. The Journalists, diminished in number, increased in respectability and independence, overlooked by a jealous and severe law, would learn to measure their expressions—they might be safely trusted. The opinion of the Chambers, the Ministers, and the public, would be mutually communicated with their proper force, and with excellent effect.

At this moment, when the 4th article of the Charter* is suspended, there is more occasion than ever for the free enunciation of the public opinion. In England, when the Habeas Corpus act sleeps, the Liberty of the Press is

* Their *Habeas corpus.*—Trans.

awake, and watches that public freedom may not sleep the sleep of death*

* We hear a great deal of the great difficulty of making a good and efficient law on the subject of the Press: there are, I admit, difficulties, but I think them not insurmountable. I have determined views upon the subject, which, however, the limits of this work do not permit me to explain.

CHAPTER XXI.

THE LIBERTY OF THE PRESS AS IT MAY AFFECT MINISTERS.

"THE freedom of the press will harass and distract the Administration: every body will write, every body will advise; and between praise, and projects, and libels, there will be no means of carrying on the Government."

All this is mighty plausible: but Ministers sincerely constitutional can never wish us to risk the state, in order to spare their *feelings*—such men will not sacrifice the dignity of their stations and their nature, to the smarts or itchings of a miserable vanity—they will not disgrace a free Monarchy with the punctilious jealousies and paltry despotism of an aristocracy. "In aristocracies," savs Montesquieu, "the magistrates are little princes, not high "enough to look down upon libels; a shaft "aimed at a monarch on the elevation of "his throne, falls short of him, but, a poor "little aristocratic lord it pierces through and "through."

I beg Ministers to recollect that they are not little aristocratic lords; they are the constitutional servants of a constitutional King. An able Minister does not disregard, but he does not fear, the freedom of the press—it attacks him, but he survives.

To be sure, Ministers will have some journals against them—well: others will be for them—they will be attacked, they will be defended, like their brethren in London.

Is the British Ministry disturbed by the jokes of the opposition, or the abuse of the Morning Chronicle? What has not been said, what not written, against Mr. Pitt? was his power diminished by it, and is his glory eclipsed?

One thing I must concede; the Liberty of the Press would render it necessary that Ministers should be men of talents and character, that they should be able to get the majority of the Chambers and the public on their side. Good writers will not then be wanting in their interests: and the journals, well written and widely circulated, will give them an honest support. They will be ten times as strong as they now are, for they will gather the public sentiment about them. When they no longer oppose themselves to the current of opinion, and stand up like exceptions to the feeling of the country, they may smile at the petty reproaches which journalists may cast upon them.

I also beg to observe that Governments are

not constituted for the exclusive use or profit of Ministers—There are others also, who have some little interest in them. If our Ministers dislike the annoyance which the freedom of the press may produce, they should go live elsewhere; a free government can never please them; for without the Liberty of the Press there can be no constitutional freedom.

A final and not unimportant consideration for Ministers is, that the Liberty of the Press relieves them from an irksome responsibility to foreign powers. They would be no longer pestered with those diplomatic notes which the negligence of a censor, or the ignorance of editors, now bring down upon them; and being no longer obliged to give way to such representations, they will no longer be obliged to degrade the dignity of their sovereign and the nation.

CHAPTER XXII.

THE CHAMBER OF DEPUTIES SHOULD NOT FRAME THE BUDGET.

The Chamber of Deputies will then, it is to be hoped, vindicate its rights and its dignity—it will demand, with the least possible delay, the freedom of the press.

That is what it ought to do: *here* is what it ought not to do—it ought not to meddle with framing the budget, this belongs essentially to the royal prerogative.

If the budget proposed by ministers is not satisfactory—reject it.

If it is good in parts, accept it in parts; but do not charge yourselves with the duty of finding taxes to replace those you reject—of substituting your own systems of finance for those of the Minister—for this reason:

The Chamber would thus pledge and embarrass itself. The Minister, whose budget you have rejected, will be no very warm partisan of yours. He may, by an extraordinary effort of virtue, do his duty, without attending to the suggestions of mortified vanity; but it is more probable that he would clog the action, and defeat the objects of your system; and then, next session, with a sly air of suppressed triumph, he would acquaint you that you had framed an admirable budget, which, however, *malheureusement*, had totally failed.

The Deputies will reply, "our budget was, perhaps, not good; but at least it was not so bad as yours;"—"Agreed," rejoins the Minister; "but yet there is a frightful deficit: do not however blame me—'tis all your own doing, and no affair of mine."

The course should be this; the Ministry prepares the budget, the Deputies sanction it: if the latter make it, they cannot punish its failure, and the Minister thus ceases to be responsible for the most important part of his duty; and so, again, the first elements of the Constitution are confounded.

But all these deviations from the strict line of the Constitution—all this agitation—these hitches and shocks in the state machine, arise, like all the difficulties of the late session, from the Ministry's struggle against the *majority*. If the Minister will return to just principles—if he proposes a budget, for which the majority can vote—all will go smoothly; and we shall be astonished at the good order, and I may, say silence, in which business will be transacted.

Having thus given my opinion on the Royal Prerogative, the House of Peers, and the Chamber of Deputies, I now come to the Ministers.

CHAPTER XXIII.

THE MINISTRY UNDER A REPRESENTATIVE MONARCHY—ITS ADVANTAGES—ITS CHANGES.

It is an incalculable advantage of a representative monarchy, that it cannot fail to bring to the head of affairs the ablest men in the state, and to endow the cabinet with, as it were, hereditary ability *.

The reason is obvious: a weak Minister could not stand before the Chambers; his errors, exposed in debate, reported in the journals, exhibited to the public, would soon effect his downfal.

I should not, therefore, in a representative government, look for any more recondite cause of the dismissal of Ministers: when the changes are frequent, it arises either from some false step of the Cabinet itself, or from ignorance of the state of the public mind, or from their general incapacity.

In an absolute monarchy frequent changes are alarming, because they may prove either a want of discernment in the Monarch, or the success of court intrigues.

* *Reflexions Politiques.*

Under a constitutional monarchy, the Ministry must and ought to be changed till the fit men are found—till the Chambers and the public shall have *forced* men of talents into eminence and power. Such changes are only the fluctuation of water which seeks its level: the oscillation of the balance before it finds its equipoise.

Until, therefore, the Ministry and the *majority* of the legislators are agreed, these changes must be expected.

CHAPTER XXIV.

THE MINISTRY SHOULD BE CREATED BY PUBLIC OPINION AND THE MAJORITY OF THE CHAMBERS.

It follows, that under a constitutional Monarchy, public opinion is the legitimate source and principle of and aministration—*principium et fons*;—and that, consequently, Ministers should spring, as it were, out of the majority of the Chamber of Deputies, which is the organ of the popular feeling.

Ministers should be members of either Chamber; because, representing a portion of the public opinion, they estimate it better, and respect it more. The Minister, who is also a Deputy, becomes impregnated with the spirit of the Chamber; which, in return—from habit and fellow-feeling—attaches itself to him.

CHAPTER XXV.

COMPOSITION OF A MINISTRY—IT OUGHT TO BE UNITED—WHAT IS MEANT BY UNITED.

The Ministry should be one.

I do not mean that the political differences of eminent men, while in private stations, are to prevent their uniting to form an Administration. They may make what they call in England a *coalition*—previously agreeing on general principles, and arranging a common plan of operation by such mutual sacrifices, as the public opinion, or the state of affairs may require or justify ;—but once assembled in Cabinet, they should thenceforward have but *one* mind.

Nor do I mean that individual Ministers should not be displaced ; I only require that their successors should bring into the Cabinet identity of interests and feelings—that the new and the old should still become *one*. In England nothing is more frequent than partial changes in the Administration ; it is the dismissal of the Prime Minister only which marks the fall of the whole.

CHAPTER XXVI.

THE MINISTRY SHOULD BE NUMEROUS.

The Ministry should be composed of a greater number of responsible advisers than it is at present; there are offices the labours of which exceed the physical strength of any individual.

The advantages of enlarging the responsible Cabinet are, 1st, the obvious facility of doing business by dividing the labour;

2d, the increasing the number of the friends and adherents of the Ministry;

3d, the lessening the spirit of intrigue, by affording many and fair objects of ambition.

CHAPTER XXVII.

THE QUALITIES OF A MINISTER.

THE first requisite of the Minister of a representative Government is a certain power of public speaking.

Not, that he requires "that highsounding "and notable eloquence, the hand-maid of "seditions, full of disobedience; rash and "arrogant, not tolerable in well constituted "States,"*—and *not*, that facility of elocution does not often accompany a very poor intellect; but at least a Minister should be able to explain himself, to reply readily to his opponents, to recapitulate with precision and force, but without bombast or declamation, the objects of the proposition he may have made. This, however, like every thing else, may be acquired by practice.

A Minister should also possess temper and conciliation; shrewdness in discovering the characters of mankind, and art in managing them. Above all, he should be firm, bold, decided in the measures he has once deliberately adopted.

Without this decision he will have no followers—nobody will defer to him who defers to all mankind.

**Dutillet.*

CHAPTER XXVIII.

WHICH FOLLOWS FROM THE PRECEDING.

Such a Minister will be at no loss to discover the feeling of the Chambers—and all Chambers will not have the same feeling, nor be gained by the same attentions.

The present assembly, for instance, is sensitive and delicate, ready to revolt at the lightest appearance of injustice or dishonour.

You might gain over its leaders and its orators;—it would not follow them: the majority would not change, because its opposition is an opposition of conscience and not of party; but talk to this Chamber in the tone of religion and loyalty,—talk to it of God, the King, their country,—it is yours.

Instead of calumniating, court it; not with words only, but by measures. It is the height of folly to hope to obtain its support while you utter to it language and doctrines which it abhors.

Do you wish to obtain from its members some concession towards what you call *revolutionary interests?*

Take care how you go about it: no apology or praise of these interests—but tell them that a fatal necessity presses upon you,—that the safety of the state requires these new sacrifices, —that you regret it,—that it is lamentable—but that it will soon be over. If they believe you, if they think you sincere, you may succeed; —but if you, on the contrary, set out with telling them that nothing can be more *just* than your proposal, and that they cannot give too many pledges for the maintenance of all the revolutionary reliques—you will have your speeches for your pains!

An English Minister has an easier task:—at Westminster every body goes directly to his object, according to his interests or his party: in France, the patronage of the Crown is not every thing. The oppositions in the two countries are not composed of the same elements. Civility will here obtain for you what a place would not; attentions will acquire what a fortune could not * buy. You must learn the tone

* M. de Chateaubriand seems to think that France differs from England in a particular which would be much to the honour of France. We flatter ourselves that if he knew us a little better, he would think that even in England places and pensions are not every thing to all men; and we believe the advice he gives to French Ministers in this chapter would be equally useful to English statesmen, if, in fact, experience,

and manners of society. The power of a French Minister is in his drawing-room as well as in his cabinet.

good sense, and good manners had not *already* taught *us* what M. de Chateaubriand is endeavouring to teach *his* countrymen.—*Trans.*

CHAPTER XXIX.

WHO NEVER CAN BE A MINISTER IN A CONSTITUTIONAL MONARCHY.

WHENEVER discussions are public, there are men of a certain character who never can be placed at the head of the Government—a speech, a jest, would suffice to overthrow such a Minister.

This check, which essentially exists in a free representative Government, was forgotten when, under a combination of delusions, (as I shall show presently,) a too famous *personage was, in spite of the too just repugnance of the crown, forced into the Cabinet.

The advancement of this man must necessarily have produced one or other of two results—the abolition of the Chamber, or the fall of the whole administration, on the first day of the session.

Can one conceive the Minister, to whom I allude, assisting in the Chamber of Deputies,

* Joseph Fouché, ci-devant of Nantes, now of Otranto. —*Trans.*

at the debate on the Categories*, or at that relative to the † 21st of January, 1793, and liable every moment to be addressed by some deputy from Lyons, by that terrible apostrophe, —"THOU ART THE MAN?"

A minister of this sort can only be ostensibly employed with the mutes of the seraglio of Bajazet, or the mutes of the senate of Buonaparte.

* The act for *classing* the revolutionary criminals, and selecting some for punishment.—*Trans.*

† The murder of the King, for which Fouché voted with cold-blooded pertinacity.—*Trans.*

CHAPTER XXX.

THE MINISTRY OF POLICE—ITS INCOMPATIBILITY WITH THE CONSTITUTION.

As there are men who cannot be Ministers under a legitimate Monarchy, so there are Ministers who ought not to exist under a constitutional Government. Need I designate the Minister of General Police?

If the Charter, which professes to secure individual liberty, is obeyed, the General Police can have neither power nor object.

If a transitory law should suspend this article of our Charter, the General Police is surely not necessary to execute this law.

And if no such suspension exists, if our rights are in full force, and that yet the General Police takes those arbitrary steps, which belong to its peculiar character, such as suppression of publications, domiciliary visits, nocturnal searches, arrests, imprisonment, exile—the Charter is annihilated.

"Oh, but the Police will not take these steps"—Then it is useless.

This General Police is in fact a political Police, a party engine; its chief tendency is to

stifle the public opinion, if it cannot disguise it —to stab, in short, the constitution to the heart. Unknown under the old regime—incompatible with the new—it is a monster born of anarchy and despotism, and bred in the filth of the revolution.

CHAPTER XXXI.

THE MINISTER OF GENERAL POLICE IS MISPLACED IN THE CHAMBER OF DEPUTIES.

The Minister of General Police is in the Chamber of Deputies—What does he there?

What a bitter irony is the word LIBERTY in *his* mouth, who, at the end of his eulogies on freedom, can arbitrarily and illegally arrest any of his Majesty's subjects!

—What a farce is a speech on the budget from *him*, who levies taxes at his own pleasure!

—What a legislator is this official protector of gaming-houses, brothels, and all the sinks into which the Police rakes for its livelihood!

—Can debates be free in presence of a bashaw who listens to them only to mark the man, whom he may at leisure denounce and strike, if he cannot corrupt?

Such are the noble functions of this office!

We affect to establish a free and constitutional Government, and we do not see that we are reviving the blessed institutions, and consecrating the tender mercies of Buonaparte.

CHAPTER XXXII.

TAXES LEVIED BY THE POLICE.

I HAVE said that the Police levies taxes not sanctioned by law; these imposts are, a tax on gaming, and a tax on newspapers*.

The gambling-houses are farmed out; their produce fluctuates; it at present produces five millions (about £250,000 sterling), per annum.

The tax on newspapers, though not so odious, is not less arbitrary.

The Charter says, Art. 47, "The Chamber of Deputies is to receive all propositions for taxes;" and Art. 48, "No tax can be enforced or levied till it has been voted by the two Chambers, and sanctioned by the King."

I am not so ignorant of human affairs as not to know that gaming-houses have been tolerated in modern society; but between mere toleration and high protection there is a wide difference: between the obscure fee given under

* There is also a tax on *prostitutes*; but the profits do not go to the General Police.

the old regime to some conniving clerk, and a revenue of five or six millions, levied arbitrarily by a Minister who renders no account,—and all this, forsooth, under a constitutional monarchy !

CHAPTER XXXIII.

OTHER UNCONSTITUTIONAL ACTS OF THE POLICE.

The Police, thus meddling with taxation, falls within the provisos of the 56th article of the Charter as swindlers or peculators. But with what is it that it does not meddle?

We find it in our Criminal Proceedings,—we see it there attacking the first principles of judicial impartiality, as we have just seen that it attacks the first principles of political order.

The 64th article of the Charter has these words: "Trials in all criminal matters shall be PUBLIC, unless where publicity may be dangerous to the state or to public morals; and in this latter case the tribunal shall, previously to closing its doors, PASS A JUDGMENT TO THIS EFFECT."

But if one of the agents of the police happens to be involved in a criminal affair, as having been a voluntary accomplice with the intention of becoming an informer—if in the course of the trial the accused should adduce in their defence this fact, which tends to their exculpation by diminishing the credit due to a character thus doubly infamous—the Police forbids the newspapers to report these parts of the evidence!

Thus complete publicity exists only against the accused; and thus an important ingredient in the cause is concealed from the public; whose opinion the law would introduce as an assistant to, or a check on, the conduct of the tribunals; and all the world (except the half dozen persons who attended the trial,) remains ignorant whether the criminal is the guilty cause of his own misfortunes, or whether he is the pitiable, if not pardonable, victim of a conspiracy of the *Police itself* against his liberty or life;—

And yet we talk of a Charter*!

* It is a singular circumstance that the case which M. de Chateaubriand so forcibly instances should have received a striking confirmation in London, even while he was writing. If the public papers had been forbidden to report the dealings of Vaughan and his associates, would they have been brought to justice, and would not several victims of their villainy have suffered on the gallows for the silence of the press?—*Trans.*

. . . .

CHAPTER XXXIV.

THE GENERAL POLICE IS OF NO REAL USE.

The General Police ought to have great advantages to redeem its illegality and danger: and yet the evidence of experience proves it to be wholly useless.

What important conspiracy has it ever detected or prevented, even under the lynx-eyed and jealous despotism of Buonaparte? This poor Police could not prevent, on the 3d Ni vose, General Mallet from sending* Pasquier and Savary (the Police itself personified,) to their own jails.

Under the King it permitted a tremendous conspiracy to wind itself round the throne—it saw nothing—it knew nothing. Napoleon's dispatches travelled regularly through the post-offices; the couriers who wore the King's livery were in the usurper's service; the two L'Allemands marched about with troops and bag-

* The Grand Judge and Minister of Police at the time when General Mallet made his strange attempt, which had at first such strange success, and which was at last so strangely defeated.—*Trans.*

gage: the Nain Jaune talked boldly of "*Plumes de Cannes**" Buonaparte had already *alighted* at that place, and still this sagacious Police knew nothing about it.

Since the second restoration, a whole department was in arms—the peasants formed themselves into organised bodies—they marched to attack a great town: but the General Police saw nothing—foresaw nothing—prevented nothing—discovered nothing.

The only important discoveries that were made were by the *extraordinary* Police—by chance---and by the exertions of some public spirited individuals. The General Police affects to complain of this extraordinary Police, and, for once, it is right; but its own inutility, and the terror it inspires, has created this establishment. The General Police cannot serve nor save the state; but, without good looking after, and it has the means of destroying it.

* I do not exactly understand this allusion, but presume it means feathers stuck in canes, with which the Buonapartists walked about, as a symbol that the wings of Buonaparte had wafted him to Cannes; the port at which he landed.—*Trans:*

CHAPTER XXXV.

THE GENERAL POLICE UNCONSTITUTIONAL AND USELESS; IS MOREOVER EXTREMELY DANGEROUS.

INCONSISTENT with a free Government, incapable of detecting or checking conspiracy, (even when it is not itself a party to the plot,) —what if the Police itself should be one of the conspirators? But what seems incredible, and yet is certain, is, that it may betray us, though the head of the office is himself honest.

The secrets of the state must be, in a certain degree, in the hands of this Police; it knows, then, the weak parts, and the best point of attack. An order from that office paralyses all the legal strength of the realm; nay, while the fourth article of the Charter is suspended, it may arrest all the civil and military authorities. Under its protection the malecontents may work in safety, lay their trains, and calculate the favourable moment for the explosion. While it rocks the Government to sleep, with one hand, it encourages the conspirators with the other, and informs them of what may be necessary for their purpose. It corresponds, with perfect security, under the inviolability of its official seal; and, by the number and variety of its agents, it communicates through all the ranks of society, from the closet of the monarch to the cellar of the *fédéré* *

Add to all this, that the agents of the Police are not generally men of the nicest honour and most estimable characters; some of them are even capable of any atrocity. What shall we think of an office which is obliged to employ a wretch like Perlet?—and it is too probable that Perlet is not a singularity in that department.

Good God! how can we suffer to exist, in the heart of a constitutional Monarchy, such a seraglio of despotism, such a sink of public corruption! Why, in a country, which pretends to be governed by laws, do we tolerate a department, whose nature it is to overleap or violate all laws?

Why intrust such monstrous powers to a minister, whose communications with all that is vile and depraved in society tend to blunt every good feeling, and inflame every bad; to profit by corruption, and thrive by abuses?

* The fédérés were a half-armed rabble, the dregs of the Septembrisers, whom Buonaparte, in his despair, had permitted to associate, or *federate*, as they called it, in his defence.—*Trans.*

What is a good Police? A good Police is that which bribes the servant to accuse his master; which seduces the son to betray his father; which lays snares for friendship, and man-traps for innocence.

A good Minister of Police will persecute if he cannot corrupt fidelity, lest it should reveal the turpitude of the offers which it has resisted. To reward crime, to entrap innocence—this is the whole secret of the Police!

The master of this formidable engine is the more terrible, because his power mixes itself with all the other departments: in fact, he is the *prime*, if not the *sole*, Minister. Nay, *He* may be said to be *King*, who commands the whole gendarmerie of France, and annually levies, without check or account to the people, seven or eight millions (from 350,000 to 400,000 sterling).

Thus whatever escapes the snares of the Police may be bought by its gold, and secured by its pensions. If it should meditate treason; but if its preparations be as yet incomplete; if it fear a premature discovery;—to dissipate suspicion, to give an earnest of its frightful fidelity—it invents a conspiracy, and sacrifices, to its credit and its treason, some wretches, under whose feet it has itself dug the pit-fall.

The Athenians attacked the nobles of Corcyra, who, driven out by the popular faction, had taken refuge on Mount Istoni. These men capitulated, and agreed to refer their cases to the judgment of the Athenian people; but it was stipulated, that, if any of them should attempt to escape, the convention should be considered as null. The Athenian generals happened to be in haste to sail for Sicily; and they were, at the same time, unwilling to allow to others the honour of conducting their unhappy prisoners to Athens. In concert, therefore, with the popular faction, they secretly persuaded some of these poor people to attempt to escape, and arrested them, of course, just as they were about to embark.—The convention was declared null—the prisoners were delivered to the Corcyrans, and massacred*.

Who would have expected to find that the Police had any resemblance to the Athenians?

* Thucyd.

CHAPTER XXXVI.

MEANS OF LESSENING THE DANGER OF THE GENERAL POLICE, IF IT BE STILL MAINTAINED.

"But are we to have no Police at all?"—I do not say that; but the evil, if it be a necessary one, ought to be diminished as much as possible.

The General Police should be confided to the magistrates, and should emanate directly from the laws. The Minister of Justice, the Attorney-general, are the natural agents of the Police: a *lieutenant de police* at Paris would complete the system.

The information from the departments will then come from the Prefect to the Minister for the Home Department, and he will communicate what may be necessary to the Minister of Justice—the Prefects will thus be freed from the trouble of a double correspondence—with the Police and the Home Department. At present, if they report the same facts to both offices, it is lost labour; if they state them differently, or in a different point of view, as the Ministers may wish to see them, it is a great evil.

So much for the Minister of Police: let us return to the administration in general.

CHAPTER XXXVII.

PRINCIPLES WHICH A CONSTITUTIONAL MINISTER SHOULD ADOPT.

WHAT are the general principles on which an administration should act?

The first and most indispensable is, that it should frankly adopt the political system under which it engages itself; submit to the personal inconvenience it may impose, and not impede its operations.

Thus, for instance, if the forms of the constitution are in some cases tedious, a Minister should not shew a fretful impatience.

—If the Chambers are to be consulted, it should be with judicious attention and decent respect, and not with the affectation or the reality of arrogance.

—If a member, in his place, should make a severe observation on a Minister, the latter should not think that France is therefore undone, and that the nation is ruined because he is laughed at.

—If a Peer or a Deputy, in the heat of debate, should drop some intemperate expressions—

nay, if he has advanced unconstitutional doctrine—Ministers should not immediately, with a terrified credulity, imagine that there is a conspiracy against the Charter, and that all is lost, or about to be lost.

These accidents will occur in the heat of public debate, and are inseparable from it. When six or seven hundred men have the privilege of speaking, and a whole nation that of writing, one must expect to hear and read abundance of trash; to be angry on such occasions is weak, childish, and quite as absurd as the nonsense of which you complain.

CHAPTER XXXVIII.

CONTINUATION OF THE SAME SUBJECT.

The Ministry—accustomed to our former constitutions, founded in the falsest doctrines, and walking hand in hand with irreligion—has been weak enough to imagine that those who advocated the cause of piety and morals were secretly undermining the Charter. Fools! as if religion and liberty were incompatible; as if every high and generous public feeling were not intimately connected with reverence for the principles of justice and of christianity.

"Oh, but they are afraid of *reaction.*" By this word they mean, I presume, *vengeance;* but to blame what is blameable, to endeavour to repair the mischief that is reparable—is that vengeance?—it is at least a noble one!

But let us take care how we permit them to use this word *reaction*, and let us distinguish there are two sorts of *reaction;* one we may call a physical or *practical* reaction, the other a *moral* reaction.

Now, all *practical* reaction, that is, all personal violence, all corporeal punishment, should be repressed. Situated as we are, Ministers cannot be too strict on this point.

But how can they, and why should they endeavour to check *moral* reaction? Can they forbid to feel, to think? Can they restrain the public opinion from branding with its scorn that which is contemptible? Not only they cannot do this, but, in any view of their duty, they ought not. To assail false doctrines, to advance the rights of justice—to encourage suffering virtue, to reward persecuted fidelity, are offices as dear to liberty as to royalty.

And would they persuade us that the men of the Revolution can be more attached to the Charter than the Royalists?—The men of the Revolution!!! They who professed the wildest theories of liberty under the Republic, they who practised the most abject baseness under Buonaparte—what common principle can they find in the Charter?—they find there a KING whom as republicans they hate, and FREEDOM, which as slaves they abhor.

Does the Ministry think the Charter much the safer for being in the custody of those men, and of the disciples of another school, which I must now mention?

This school professes the stale doctrine of passive obedience, denies all power to the Chambers, and would perform all the functions of legislation and government by *Royal ordonnances*. Whenever such doctrines have been advanced, the Royalists have always boldly resisted them—witness the law of elections—and have strenuously repelled the principles of passive obedience, preached up by the very men who, under the cloak of liberty, had so lately overturned the throne and the state.

If, then, Ministers believe, that in a country where there is liberty of speech, they can avoid hearing opinions of all colours—and if they take individual assertions as indications of general feeling, or of premeditated system—I tell them they know nothing about a representative government, and they will fall into pitiable absurdities by acting upon their own vague suspicions and irritable humour.

The true rule on such occasions is—not to weigh a hasty word, or measure some insulated assertion, but—to weigh and measure consequences and facts. A statesman should think only of the result such things may have. If they lead to no practical mischief, they do no real harm; if they lead to good, it is of little consequence whether they spring from prejudice or reason, from chance or judgment. In politics, if we once stray away from the guidance of *facts*, we shall bewilder ourselves irretrievably.

CHAPTER XXXIX.

MINISTERS SHOULD LEAD OR FOLLOW THE MAJORITY.

MINISTERS should, in their administration of affairs, defer to the public opinion signified to them by the majority of the Deputies.

This opinion may not be theirs: their tastes, their habits, their inclinations may lead them a contrary way: but they must then either alter the opinion of the majority, or submit to it. Without the majority they cannot go on.

I shall state, hereafter, how we have fallen into the political heresy that an administration can go on with the support of a minority only. It was the device of a moment of despair, to justify false systems and imprudent pledges.

If it be said "that ministers may remain in power in spite of a majority"—because the majority cannot actually seize by the collar and turn them bodily out o' doors—it is true enough—but if to suffer every hour the most degrading humiliation—if to hear in every speech the bitterest reproaches—if to be in a constant doubt of the success of all one's measures—if *this* be to keep one's place, then all I can say is, that the Minister remains, but the Government goes.

There is no medium in a constitution like ours: the Minister *must* lead or follow the majority; if he will not or cannot do either, he must dissolve the Chambers, or resign; but it is for him to consider whether he has the courage to risk (even eventually) the safety of the nation in order to keep his place—whether he has strength to strike such a blow—whether he can answer for the tranquillity of the country during the elections—whether he is sure he can direct the choice of the electors, or finally, whether being sure of none of these, he had not better either resign at once, or reconcile himself with the majority.

In this latter case he had better make haste, for it is not so certain that a majority—long thwarted and insulted by such a Minister—will be ready to embrace him whenever he mav choose to throw them the handkerchief.

CHAPTER XL.

MINISTERS SHOULD ATTEND THE SITTINGS.

ANOTHER heresy---" Ministers, it is said, are not obliged to attend in the Chambers the discussion of their own measures."

This is a continuation of the same principle which I reprobated before*, that " a Minister is not obliged to account to the Chambers for his conduct,"—" that he is responsible only to the King," &c. &c.

All these positions are absolutely untenable, and contrary to the essence of a representative government. If a Minister will not condescend to defend his own measures, who will? Can business be done by arrogance and ill-humour? Why is one a Minister but to do the work of a Minister? And what higher duty can he have than to attend in Parliament and share in its debates? What? he thinks it more important to shut himself up in his cabinet, to work upon some little miserable detail, than to watch over and guide the great measures of law and policy on which the safety of the whole people depends!

* Chapter XV.

If the Chambers should adopt a similar course, and should treat the measures of the Ministers only as cavalierly as the Ministers themselves do, what would become of us?

Get back to the high road of common sense —reconcile yourselves with the majority, and you will feel no repugnance at appearing in an assembly where you will receive nothing but support, and hear nothing but expressions of confidence.

But ill-temper and false systems will spoil and ruin all.

CHAPTER XLI.

THE THREE MINISTRIES, SINCE THE RESTORATION, ALL IN THE SAME ERROR.

But what do I mean by *false systems?*

I mean whatever is essentially contrary to the principle of existing institutions; whatever leads to its own inevitable dissolution.

Since the restoration, one great and fatal error has been invariably pursued; the successive administrations have walked in the same path—with no other variation than the little which their personal dispositions occasioned—and with different degrees of celerity, according to the degree of opposition which they found in their own cabinets.

Before I examine these systems themselves, it is necessary to say a word or two of each of the three administrations, by whom these systems have been so unfortunately brought into vogue.

CHAPTER XLII.

THE FIRST CABINET.

WHEN in 1814 the Minister for foreign affairs (M. de Talleyrand) set out for Vienna, he left behind him a very well bred and even pleasant cabinet, but totally unfit for business; and bringing to it that sort of pettishness which one feels at finding his reputation slipping from under him.

When a Minister is in this situation, he is ready for any change of system—terrified at the responsibility—soured by that sort of opposition, which, in such circumstances, meets him at every turn—destitute of the means of controlling events and measures—and feeling that he is carried off by a torrent, he becomes disgusted with the trouble of governing —lays the blame every where but at home—attributes his own failure to the nature of our institutions, to public bodies, to private individuals; in short, to any body but himself; and, full of criticism and imbecility, ruins France in the name of the Charter.

This is a sketch of the historv of the first administration. It proposed no law of restraint, but that impolitic one against the press—it foresaw no danger, and would not listen to those who did.

When it was advised to do so or so—however just or necessary the measure—the eternal answer was, "'tis against the Charter;" a good answer, if it were true.

The Cabinet very soon became divided, and was still further weakened by this division.

It was in the majority of this Cabinet that this new doctrine was first broached, that the Chambers are only the King's council—that, in fact, the government is not representative—that all comparisons between France and England are ridiculous—that we can go on very well without laws, and do all that we have to do by way of *ordonnances*.

The Buonapartists readily adopted this commentary on the Charter; it was at least impolitic, and might therefore lead to new disturbances, and they desired, of course, no better—or it might, if acquiesced in, re-establish a despotism, after which these magnanimous citizens have, in spite of their republicanism, always had a hankering; so that, either way, *they* were satisfied.

When one has sense enough to know that he is gone wrong, but too much vanity to confess it, he invariably plunges deeper into his error—it is the course and consolation of self-love. The Ministry grew angry.

When we criticised a bad appointment, or proposed a royalist for a favour of the crown, they told us, "No, we shall give it to any clever Buonapartist who will take it." There was, of course, no want of Buonapartites; and of course Buonaparte returned!

By degrees this administration found out that no man could have talents who had not taken part in the revolution; and this doctrine, transmitted from cabinet to cabinet, is now an undeniable article of political faith.

And yet the majority of the very cabinet which established this doctrine included several excellent royalists—men well known for their generous efforts against the revolution—of the most upright conduct, the purest morals, and the highest honour—who had never bent the knee to any revolutionary Baal. It was therefore their own sentence that they pronounced. Having nobly stood aloof from the contamination of revolutionary office, they declared themselves unfit to be ministers; and in this instance, it must be confessed, that their example justified their theory.

What is more common than to see defeated vanity take steps the most contrary to its own interests? For instance, every statesman who commits an error now-a-days, every dismissed politician, joins immediately the revolutionary faction—their mortified vanities make assignations, and meet one another in that great sanctuary of crime and folly.

There we see assembled all the survivors of those who have appeared on the stage from 1789 to 1816. Differing, no doubt, in a thousand circumstances, they all agree in one—they are dissatisfied with themselves and every body else; and they club together, into one stock of discontent, the vain regrets of imbecility, and the keener remorse of crime.

CHAPTER XLIII.

MEASURES OF THE FIRST CABINET.

This cabinet, however, was after all too intelligent to think it could go on without a majority of the Chambers;—it had it, and made no use of it.

Only one important law, that against the Press, was proposed: and for that the most puerile reasons were adduced—such as delicacy towards the fair sex; respect to the royal authority (that is to the Minister), &c.—but general or constitutional reasoning there was none. Indeed why should those think it worth while to adduce arguments to an assembly which they considered as a mere passive, unprivileged, and mechanical council?

After all, the law had no effect, except to cast odium on the government, and ensure impunity to the licentiousness of the Press.

It produced also but one remarkable *ordonnance*, which—professing to regulate public education—threw the whole subject into confusion.

The Chambers had a great advantage over the Ministry; the propositions originating with the former were as judicious as those of the latter were silly or mischievous. The best, the noblest, the most enlarged view of public affairs taken in that session, was by a marshal of France.

The first administration was soon overthrown by a storm which it might have prevented—and France was nearly overthrown with it.

CHAPTER XLIV.

THE SECOND CABINET.

The Prime* Minister of the first cabinet was placed, by common consent, at the head of the second. The fairest field was open before him—he had now the power of completing his work, and of consolidating the throne, in the restoration of which he had so powerfully assisted. He had only to appreciate justly his own situation,—to renounce sincerely the revolution and its men,—to adopt cordially the principles of a constitutional Monarchy founded in religion, morality, and justice,—to select for the public service men of irreproachable character and known attachment to the crown and the state.

The name of this minister—his talents—his knowledge of business—his reputation in Europe—all conspired to call him to this high trust, which might have been alike glorious to him and useful to his country. He would have gone down to posterity with the double glory

* M. de Talleyrand.

of those extraordinary men who overthrow and re-establish nations. The splendour of his fame would have silenced envy and even memory.

Naturally inclined to this course by exalted birth, and extraordinary sagacity, he was diverted from it by one of those fatalities which break the line of reason and nature, and change unexpectedly the destinies of man.

Too long absent from France, he did not understand the true state of the national mind; he was obliged to enquire of others, and they deceived him; for with all his genius and sagacity, he is perhaps a better judge of business than of men. He therefore returned—almost in spite of himself—into trammels, which he felt he ought to throw off.

CHAPTER XLV.

CONTINUATION.

THESE false systems received a strange reinforcement by the appointment to the Ministry of a man* who had ventured to remain in Paris.

This famous person had at first avoided committing himself—he wished to have two strings to his bow; and he who sent little messages to Ghent probably sent others of a different colour elsewhere.

As we advanced into France we found that a powerful coalition was formed in his favour; when we approached Paris we found it irresistible. Every body was in it. Religion, impiety, virtue, vice, the royalist, the republican, the allies, and the French. I never saw so extraordinary a mania: we heard from all sides that without *this* Minister there was neither hope for the King, nor peace for France; that *he alone* had prevented a great battle under the walls of Paris, and saved the capital, and that *he alone* could finish his great work.

Let me be forgiven if I here say one word of

* Fouché.—*Trans.*

myself. I would not now state what I then thought if my sentiments were not already public. I maintained then, in the midst of all this mad enthusiasm, that no event, that no argument could justify such an appointment; that if ever he became Minister he would ruin France, or be dismissed in three months. My prediction has been accomplished.

Besides the moral reasons which led me to this conclusion, two others appeared unanswerable.

In politics, as in every thing else, we should first enquire what is possible. The proposed appointment appeared to me to involve two impossibilities.

The first arose out of the peculiar situation in which this Minister was placed in relation to the King.

The second arose out of the constitutional objection which is stated in the 39th chapter of this work.

If it were thought that the services of such a man could be useful, he should have been placed behind the curtain; consulted, counselled with in secret; liberally rewarded by riches for himself, and advancement for his family; but the shock which his public appointment gave to loyal feeling and to the dignity of the Monarch ought to have been spared; but I will at the same time confess that it is almost impossible, even to the best judgments, to resist the pressure of circumstances and the delusion of the moment.

I shall never forget the pang I suffered at St. Denis. It was about nine o'clock in the evening,—I had remained in the King's antichamber,—the door opened; the Prince of Talleyrand entered, leaning on the arm of— M. Fouché.—Oh, Louis the Desired! Oh, my unhappy master! You have *indeed* shown that there is no sacrifice which your people may not expect from your paternal tenderness!

. . . .

CHAPTER XLVI.

FIRST STEP OF THE SECOND MINISTRY.

THE new Cabinet thus installed, must do something; and their new ally, of course, proposed the only step consistent with his interest. *His* ministerial existence was incompatible, he felt, with the course of a representative monarchy. He understood perfectly, that if the illegitimate armed force, and the illegitimate political powers, were not alike preserved, his fall was inevitable. He knew that there is no struggling with the force of facts and things; and as he could not identify himself with the elements of a legal monarchy, he wished to render the principles of the government consistent with his own.

He well nigh succeeded. He had created a fictitious terror before the Court entered Paris: he endeavoured, by a detail of imaginary dangers, to oblige the King to recognise the two Chambers—the rump of Buonaparte—and to accept a certain *declaration of rights,* at which certain philosophers, tailors of his sect, were working night and day, in order that it might be ready in time to throw over the King's shoulders at his entry into his capital. Louis XVIII. would then have been *King* by the constitutions of the *empi e*—the people would have been so good as to elect him for Chief Magistrate—his acts would have been dated the first year of his reign—the body and Swiss guards would have been cashiered—the army of the Loire preserved—and the white cockade would have been torn from the faithful soldiers who had followed their King into his exile, and now accompanied him back to the palace of his ancestors—to make way for the tricoloured symbol of a rebellion, which was even yet in arms against its legitimate sovereign.

This would have been indeed the consummation of the Revolution: the royal family might then have been tolerated at Paris for a certain period, till, some fine day, the sovereign people, and the still more sovereign Ministers, should think proper to dismiss their monarch and abolish the monarchy: nay, at this epoch, the revolutionary faction was heard to mutter something about the necessity of *exiling* the Princes of the blood. The King was to be isolated from his family, and the throne was to be solitary confinement in a workhouse.

CHAPTER XLVII.

CONTINUATION.

In the mean while the system of terror and dupery went on.

The warmest Royalists hurried out, with ridiculous sincerity, to inform us, that if the King ventured to enter Paris with the household troops, we should all be massacred; that if we did not all mount the tricoloured cockade, we should see a general insurrection. In vain did the national guards *climb over* the walls of Paris to assure the King of their devotion; we were told that the national guards were exasperated against us. The faction had shut the barriers to prevent the people from flying to meet their Sovereign. The conspiracy was as much against this good people as against the King. Our blindness was miraculous. The French army, the only source of danger, was in march for the Loire; one hundred and fifty thousand of the allied troops occupied the posts, the avenues, the barriers, of Paris; they were to enter the city by capitulation, within twenty-four hours; and yet they would have us believe that the King, with his guards and allies, was not strong enough to venture into a *city*, where there did not remain a single soldier, and whose loyal inhabitants (and they were, I may say, the whole population) were more than sufficient to have alone kept down a handful of rabble fédérés, if these latter had wished or dared to stir.

A circumstance occurred which might have opened our eyes: the Provisional Government was dissolved; but it left behind it a posthumous proclamation*; a kind of indictment against the legitimate Monarch and his servants. This proclamation was intended as a foundation stone—laid now, to be built on hereafter; and the edifice intended was a new revolution. This startled some of us; but *the* Minister having assured us that *this* was the only means he had of dissolving the Provisional Government, and that all was right—we believed him! Now, observe, this very Minister was *himself* the Provisional

* I myself bought in the streets of Paris copies of this proclamation, printed for the use of the people, on paper stamped with Buonaparte's eagle, in which there are some significant phrases not to be found in the Moniteur; such as, that good men, *forced* to retire, should reserve their noble and patriotic efforts and intentions *for happier times*.

Government—its body and soul; and that (but for *his* precautions) this *Directory*, which he pretended 150,000 soldiers could not subdue, might have been thrown into the river by fifty of the national guards, who had a great mind to do it.

CHAPTER XLVIII.

THIS PLAN DEFEATED.

THIS farce ended I hardly know how. The new Directory, the Peers, and the Representatives of Buonaparte, evaporated; the household troops marched quietly into Paris; the tricoloured cockade was rejected—thanks to the spirit of the heir of Henry IV. who declared, that rather than wear it, he would return to Hartwell*. The white flag again floated on the Tuilleries, and—to the great wonderment of the dupes,—never was the King more enthusiastically welcomed, or his guards more cordially received. The pretended resistance was no where to be found, and obstacles, which never existed, had no great difficulty in disappearing.

It was a little amusing to observe the amazement and shame which appeared in the faces of our *prophets*, for a short time after. Every one at first endeavoured to justify his former advice, and insisted that the choice of the new Minister was indispensible; but, by and by, when the opinions of the departments and of Europe be-

* His Majesty's late residence in England.—*Trans.*

gan to reach us (and neither Europe nor the departments were for a moment deceived), when the reign of terror began to wear out in Paris, we came back to our senses, and soon discovered (what I had foreseen) that this same Ministry which had been forced on the King, as it were by storm, ought not—could not last.

I blame nobody. It was very natural that those who had considered themselves as protected by Fouché, during the hundred days of interregnum—(but who would have been miserably deceived, had we lost the battle of Waterloo),—should be under the delusion of gratitude; but since this error, strong as it was, has been so soon exposed, it ought at least to make them more cautious for the future. When we hear them, therefore, excusing all the faults of the Ministry of to-day—when they maintain with equal confidence, that without such or such a Ministry all is lost, we beg of them to REMEMBER FOUCHE'! —their enthusiasm for this nine days wonder, their asseverations that he alone could save us—their long arguments, and their laconic ill humour against the profane few who doubted of his infallibility. They should thence learn to be a little more diffident in their judgments, and a little more reserved in the distribution of their anathemas.

CHAPTER XLIX.

DIFFERENCES IN THE SECOND CABINET.

The general revolutionary plan having failed, its author, if he had been wise, would have retired; for, as I said before, he could not assimilate himself with the legitimate system; and the revolutionary intrigue had, as we have seen, broken down under him. If this resignation had taken place, the amended Ministry might have gone on; it would not at least have been in that inconsistent predicament, which drove it to false steps, and hurried it on to its fall.

The Prime Minister (M. de Talleyrand) escaped from the torrent which had at first carried him away with so many others—was glad to return to juster principles, and to a system sincerely royal and constitutional.

For this purpose a Chamber of Deputies was indispensible, and it was convened. The electors and the Presidents of the Electoral Colleges were generally chosen from among the royalists. But this very result, favorable as it was, overthrew the administration; because it rendered still more critical the situation of the man of the revolution, and this Minister—by consenting to these measures, by persisting even in being himself elected to the Chamber of Deputies—displayed, on his part, a complete ignorance of his real situation and prospects.

By what accident did so sharp-sighted a politician become so suddenly blind? His first and great efforts having failed, he could no longer arrest the course of events; the constitution was established, and he could not stop the growth of the tree, or the natural production of its fruit; and he hoped, perhaps, to find in this Chamber some remains of a revolutionary spirit with which he might again be able to quicken into action; besides, vain and changeable, this man, whose name is immortalized in our misfortunes, bèlieved himself able to

Ride on the whirlwind and direct the storm,

because forsooth he had been so often shipwrecked, and that a levity (ill assorted with the weight of the affairs he has had to manage,) had saved him from drowning.

When Cromwell signed the death-warrant of Charles the First, he amused himself with inking the face of Martin, another regicide, to whom he was handing the pen. It is the common affectation of great offenders to bear the tortures of conscience with gaiety.

CHAPTER L.

FALL OF THE SECOND CABINET.

The acts of so discordant an administration could not but be contradictory: some of them are excellent, others deplorable, and which will entail on our institutions the most disastrous effects. Candour obliges me to confess, that if the present cabinet has been involved in inextricable difficulties, the greater part of those difficulties they inherit from their predecessors.

A single example will suffice to show how egregiously the second Ministry could be mistaken in the most important points.

The moment the reins of government were confided to it, it ought to have lost no time in bringing to justice all great criminals,—in exiling those who might be thought to deserve banishment—and in publishing a *full* and *entire amnesty* to ALL the rest: the guilty would then have been punished, and the weak would have been forgiven.

But, instead of this obvious measure, they permitted punishment and fear to hover over France. Called upon, too late, to take cognizance of these offences, the Chambers have been forced to open wounds and renew discussions to exasperate passions, and awaken recollections. Prosecutions and sentences—at once partial and unlimited—are going on even at the moment I write; and as we have seen one person convicted for the same precise offence of which others have been acquitted; this rigour and this indulgence have the appearance of mutually reproaching each other with injustice.

Dissatisfaction went on increasing: the Ministers, disunited, began to look for help in the conflicting opinions of parties. The affair of the Museum added to the general discontent. The publication of two furious *reports developed the whole of the revolutionary plan, which it had been attempted to force upon the King, and which I have already exposed: but these reports could no longer produce any effect—the day for chimerical terrors was gone by; they were now appreciated at their real value, as the last gasps of defeated ambition, and the writhings of despair:—as compositions, they were contemptible—false facts, vague objects, and a mean and rambling style.

So great a scandal, so many contradictions, so many experiments, and so many defeats, hastened the catastrophe which every one had foreseen.

* Those of Fouché.—Ed.

The session was about to commence. The very shadow of the Chambers sufficed to dissipate a Ministry which trembled by anticipation at their voice; and dared not meet them.

When these ministers were dismissed, there was no great difficulty in finding successors, though we had been so often and so strenuously assured that there were no others to be had.

CHAPTER LI.

THE THIRD CABINET—ITS MEASURES AND LAWS.

The new Ministry came into power just at the commencement of the session. The laws which they proposed were urgent and necessary: they were all adopted, though with considerable amendments.

Thus this Chamber, of which the Ministers so soon began to complain, did its duty by the King, whom it adores, and by the people, whose rights it guards. By the laws for the suspension of the * Habeas Corpus; against seditious cries; for establishing les Cours † Prevotales; on the Amnesty; it strengthened the hands of the Crown—by the amendments made to the law of elections and to the budget, it advanced the interests of the people.

If the Ministry had been contented, for its own repose and for that of France, to have followed the constitutional course, and acted with the *majority*, the labours in which they were employed, at once useful and brilliant, would

* I use the most intelligible English paraphrase for the French terms.—Ed.

† The cours prevotales are a kind of summary tribunals which partake of the military as well as the civil forms of law.

have consoled the nation for thirty years of follies and faults.

The laws proposed by the Ministry were great and useful public measures; more carefully framed, they would have passed without hesitation.

The propositions and suggestions made by the Chambers were the foundations also of great and useful measures: they were accepted by the Ministers, and perfected by the joint wisdom of both.

But the error I have above stated deranged all: the Chamber, which should have been a meeting of friends, became a field of battle.

Let us then examine this system of errors, which lost our country on the *20th of March, and which now are, and hereafter will be so extensively mischievous.

* Buonaparte's second usurpation.—*Trans.*

CHAPTER LII.

THE FOLLOWERS OF THIS SYSTEM*.

There are servants of the Crown who have embraced the revolutionary projects which have been carried on since the restoration, seeing very clearly the secret objects, and desiring very sincerely their accomplishment.

There are statesmen who have fallen into them from ignorance and error—there are others who have embraced them from personal dislike to their opponents; and others who adhere to them from pride, passion, obstinacy, or ill humour.

It is clear that these systems, like all other human opinions, have their knaves and their dupes; but as—whether knaves or fools—they drag us towards the same abyss, it is of little consequence to us what their motives may be.

Fairfax had suffered himself to be drawn on by the Parliamentarians: he saw too late that he was deluded—too late he resolved to snatch the King from the hands of his executioners. The regicide faction knew this, and commissioned Harrison to avert the danger. Harrison visited the weak and superstitious Fairfax, and persuaded him to join in prayer for light from heaven in this momentous decision: Harrison knew the hour at which the execution was to take place, and he prolonged his miserable and blasphemous canting till the blow was struck: they were still on their knees when the fatal event was announced. It is the will of heaven! exclaimed Harrison, rising suddenly. Fairfax was overwhelmed with consternation and remorse; but the King was dead!

Let us not think then of men but of measures.

If I can prove the falsehood of the principles, the danger of the projects which are now afloat—if I can warn the pilots, who now hold the helm of the state, of the shoals on which we are driving, I shall have done my duty to my country;—convinced, as I am, that if we do not alter our course, the legitimate Monarchy will be stranded and wrecked.

CHAPTER LIII.

PRINCIPAL SYSTEM—THE FOUNDATION OF THE REST.

THE principal system of government, since the restoration—the base of all the others—is that from which the following heresies are derived, viz. *there are no royalists in France—the Deputies do not represent the public opinion—the majority of the Chamber is not the organ of the nation—the royalists are incapable*, &c. &c.

This system, which can only be supported by denying the evidence of facts—by misrepresenting things—by calumniating men—by outraging common sense—by quitting the straight high road for an intricate and dangerous path: this system is, in one word, that

FRANCE OUGHT TO BE GOVERNED ON THE PRINCIPLE OF REVOLUTIONARY INTERESTS.

This uncouth phrase, well worthy its authors, is the whole instruction which a modern Minister need learn. Whoever does not understand it, is pronounced devoid of ministerial talents. He is not worth teaching; and they do not condescend to explain to him the meaning of the jargon used in the coteries of Paris, by the adepts in these high mysteries.

CHAPTER LIV.

THE CONDUCT OF THE MINISTRY EASILY EXPLAINED.

FOLLOW this system, as a clue, and it will lead you through all the recesses and intricacies of the Cabinet. You will see at once the reason of what before appeared inconceivable, and you will have the secret of the whole ministerial riddle. Now for the proof.

There are but two sorts of men who can govern France in the spirit of *revolutionary interests*—those who are themselves revolutionists; or those who believe that the majority of the nation is.

The conduct of both these classes is natural: of the first obviously so—and of the second, because, sincere, though in error, they are persuaded that all resistance would be unavailing, and could only lead to disturbance and danger; and they conceive it to be their duty to defer to a paramount and invincible public opinion.

This being once assumed, it follows that the *men* and *things* of the *revolution* are ALONE to be favored or feared, and that by a necessary consequence the men and things which do not belong to this blessed revolution should not be favored, because they are not to be feared.

Now, I ask, is not this a simple resolution of the whole enigma of the measures of Government since the restoration—Is not all now plain, all clear, all comprehensible to the meanest capacity?

But, this system of Government, has it saved—has it lost—will it lose our country?—That is now the question.

If it has saved France, it is the true system, and ought to be followed.

But if it has once already lost France, and will do so again, it is false, and let us hasten to get out of it.

Now I am ready to maintain that this system of revolutionary partialities threw us into the danger from which we are but just extricated, and will, if pursued, again lead us into an abyss, from which we shall find no redemption.

I say that it is astonishing, monstrous, that Ministers, sincere friends to the throne, should fall again into the same train which produced the 20th of March.

I say that it is inconceivable how persons of common sense can persist in sacrificing France in the hope of gaining over men whom they never can gain, and who are not worth having—how they can bewilder themselves in the vapors of this political alchymy, and hope to melt down and amalgamate what the fire and the force of Buonaparte could not unite—and how they can persuade themselves that a weapon of destruction can become—like the spear of Ituriel—a healing remedy!

I will shew you in detail,—you shall see, you shall *touch*—the terrible results of this madness; but let me first develope its principles, and that of the others derived from it.

CHAPTER LV.

THE MISTAKE OF THE HONEST SUPPORTERS OF THIS SYSTEM.

THE mistake of the honest supporters of this system is that they confound the *material* and the *moral* interests of the revolutionists. I say protect the former, but persecute, destroy, annihilate the latter.

I mean by the *material* revolutionary interests, the possession of national property, the enjoyment of political rights, sprung from the revolution, and consecrated by the Charter.

By the *moral*—or rather *immoral*—interests of the revolution, I mean anti-christian and anti-social doctrines—the principle of passive or active obedience to any and every government *de facto*—and in short whatever tends to render indifferent or praiseworthy, treachery, robbery, and injustice.

CHAPTER LVI.

HOW WE SHOULD ACT.

Be steady then in your maintenance of national property to its present proprietors, and of constitutional rights to all classes of the people —punish those who would assail either.

But it is a deplorable and odious error to extend this protection to all the impious and sacrilegious doctrines which have sprung, like Egyptian toads, from the slime of the revolutionary deluge. It is to confound real and tangible interests with pernicious and destructive theories.

CHAPTER LVII.

EXAMPLE.

For example:—because we have sold property which did not belong to us, and because the Charter (to avoid fresh disturbances,) recognises and legalises this transfer, must we therefore admit that it is legal to keep from its natural owners the property which is not yet sold? One injustice committed, and, from the necessity of the case, legalised, can it warrant another for which there is no necessity, and which is neither legal nor legalised? In restoring, for instance, to the Church the ecclesiastical property now in the hands of the government, are we afraid that it would be implied that we were wrong in selling that which is gone, and which in fact no one seeks to recover?—It is, however, an avowal of a plain truth, which must be made at last.

The doctrines of those disciples of liberty are somewhat singular.

The rights of property, established by the Charter, are construed to extend to those only who have other people's goods, and not to those who seek to obtain their own. These rights of property are made, it would seem, for *new* France, and exclude *old* France—they protect the acquisitions of yesterday, and defeat those of a thousand years ago.—Confiscation of property is abolished by the Charter in the cases of *treason;* but it is permitted to exist, it seems, in cases of *fidelity.*

Woe to the nation whose law, like the plumb-line of some Greek architects that we read of, can accommodate itself to different angles! Woe to the nation whose justice has two sets of weights and measures! Woe to the man who demands from the law what he denies to his neighbour! his prosperity will wither like grass, and he will be stricken with that same palsy of poverty which he does not pity in his fellow.

In the days of Philip of Valois there was a plague; during the mortality it happened that two monks of St. Denis, travelling across the country, arrived at a little village, where they found men, women, and children dancing to the pipe and tamborin; when the holy men asked the reason of this unseasonable merriment, the peasants replied, that their neighbours were dying around them, but that the contagion had not reached their village, so that they had hopes they should escape, and were making merry to keep up their spirits. The two monks passed on. Some time after they returned; they came to the same village; it was desolate; they asked one or two pale and dying wretches whom they saw in the street, where the men and women were who were dancing so gaily and so lately? "Fair gentlemen," replied the peasants, "the wrath of Heaven hath descended upon us*"

* Chroniques de France.

CHAPTER LVIII.

THE SAME SUBJECT CONTINUED.

Go on, and see where your system will carry you.

Of course you will have no established religion, because Christianity is not favourable to *revolutionary interests.*

No proposition tending to re-establish any of the pious or moral institutions of our ancestors must be entertained :—they might undermine *revolutionary interests*, at least they would remind us that the revolution had destroyed them, and we must not even indirectly reproach the revolution.

Have I not heard the funeral rites which were paid to Louis XVI. to the Queen, to the young King, to Madame Elizabeth, censured as impolitic? Alas, alas! Is it thus that the monarchy is to be preserved?

If from things we proceed to men, we shall again find *revolutionary interests* crossing us at every step. We must not promote a royalist,—a man who has opposed any stage of the revolution; and, on the contrary, all the friends of the revolution are to be courted and rewarded.

I shall attempt the details of this hasty sketch when I come to paint the present state of France.

In short, whoever uses the words honour, religion, loyalty—is factious; such expressions are contrary to *revolutionary interests*.

Just before the revolution, appalled and intimidated by the spirit of the times, even the preacher in the pulpit of God hardly dared pronounce the name of Jesus Christ. They endeavoured by paraphrase and circumlocution to make us understand whom they meant.

Now-a-days *revolutionary interests* command us to avoid all expressions which might offend the ear of *revolutionary dclicacy*. *Restitution*, for example, is a frightful word,—banished, it and its derivatives, from the French language. There are some good souls who would almost consent to make some small provision for the poor and humble christians who attend at the altar of God, but then it must be *given*, and not *restored* to the clergy; even though it be from the *unalienated* property of the Church; for as they say very gravely, wisely, and elegantly, "*you must stick to your principles.*"

If this goes on, *thanks to revolutionary interests*, we shall have a new dictionary, with a multitude of words no where else to be found.

CHAPTER LIX.

THE SYSTEM OF REVOLUTIONARY INTERESTS, MATERIAL AS WELL AS MORAL, LEADS TO THIS OTHER, THAT THERE ARE NO ROYALISTS IN FRANCE.

To maintain *revolutionary interests* with regard to *morals*, is so dissonant from all principles of legitimate government; it seems so absurd to caress one's enemies, and to repel one's friends, that it is necessary to allege some overwhelming argument in defence of such conduct—and what do you think they found:

THERE ARE NO ROYALISTS IN FRANCE.

Thus an error is supported by a falsehood.

"How many are you?" asked, one day, a *special** personage, "two royalists to one hundred revolutionists—submit then to your fate. *Væ Victis!* a government can recognise only the majority, and acts for it—facts, not words—come, let us count."

Well, then, let us.

You say that there are about two royalists to one hundred revolutionists; or, to use your

* This word belongs to that *jargon* alluded to at the conclusion of the 53d chapter.—*Trans.*

common expression, *there are no royalists in France*; thence you conclude, that the *revolutionary interests*—not only the material (which I grant), but the moral (which I attack)—should be maintained without distinction.

If I conceded your fact, I should deduce a contrary inference, but I begin by absolutely denying it.

CHAPTER LX.

THE MAJORITY OF FRANCE ARE ROYALISTS.

THE royalists, far from being the small minority, are the immense majority of France.

"Oh," say our opponents, "if they had been so, the Revolution never could have happened."

Pray, how long have majorities influenced revolutions? Has not experience shewn, that more frequently the minority carry all before them? Did, for instance, France desire the murder of Louis XVI.?—was she for the Convention and its crimes—for the Directory and its baseness—for Buonaparte and his conscription? She wished for none of this—her heart revolted at it all; but she was restrained by an active and armed minority. Can we then infer, because a majority is silent, that it does not exist; that its sentiments do not live in a million of hearts. If this be true there is a very short rule for all cases—the oppressed are always wrong, and the oppressor is always right.

But relieve this majority from the yoke of tyranny, and what will happen?

The answer is before our eyes.

The Electoral Colleges, summoned and composed by Buonaparte, exercise their elective functions under the King. Of which party are they? They elect the most determined royalists. I will say more:—it required the whole force of ministerial influence to procure the return of certain individuals whom the public feeling repelled.

Far from wishing for revolutionists, we are sick of them. The tide is set the other way, we desire no more revolutions, and no more revolutionists.

But let us stick to facts. I entreat my reader to call to his recollection the departments, the towns, villages, hamlets, with which he may be acquainted. In all these places he will have no difficulty in reckoning the numbers of the revolutionary men. Are there a thousand in a department, an hundred in a town, a dozen in the village or hamlet? There is no such thing.

Those who have only travelled through provinces devastated by two successive invasions—who have followed the steps of twelve hundred thousand foreign soldiers—who have heard the peasants complaining amid their plundered fields, and desolated cottages—are they to judge of the whole population by the accents of grief, of hunger, and of misery? But how is it that these very provinces have returned deputies at least as royalist as the rest of France? Can we be ignorant that all the northern departments are animated by the purest loyalty? In the west and south the fervour of this feeling amounts to enthusiasm.

These are facts.

CHAPTER LXI.

WHAT HAS DECEIVED THE MINISTRY AS TO THE REAL SENTIMENTS OF THE PEOPLE.

The delusion of Ministers on the real state of the public mind is connected also with another cause. They mistake for external, what is really internal, and are amazed to see in the public mind what exists only in their own.

Ministers forget that they collect the general opinion through very narrow and contracted organs. The majority of places were, and still are, in the hands of the revolutionists or Buonapartists. Ministers correspond only with these placemen: they ask them for information as to the opinion of France, and these men give their own; and they assure the Ministry that all mankind are of their mind, except only a handful of Chouans and Vendéans. Count up the army of custom-house and excise officers, of all ranks of functionaries, of all classes of clerks, you will find they are all in the *revolutionary interest*.

If, then, indeed, the opinion of France is to

be judged, not by that of the people, but by that of the agents of Government, certainly there are very few royalists; and as it is the sort of gentry I have just mentioned who talk and write, who guide the journals, and make fame as an organ grinder makes music, by the machine which they work; they form the public voice, and it is not surprising that they deceive their employers—they deceive themselves.

CHAPTER LXII.

THIS OBJECTION REFUTED.

A MAN of sagacity, who was asked what the public opinion of France was, begun by saying that "the royalists were the best sort of people in the world, full of zeal and devotion"—(this is the approved form for beginning to libel us). He then added, "but these worthy people are unluckily so few in number, of so little consideration as a party, that they were not able, on the 20th of March, to save the King at Paris, or the Duchess at Bordeaux."

Good God! who, then, are they who use such an argument to prove the minority of the royalists?—are they not the very men who endeavour to excuse events in which they see their own condemnation?—worthy public servants, the authors and favourers of the system of *revolutionary interests*, by which none are to be promoted but the friends of Buonaparte—the disciples of the Revolution?

What, YOU, who would believe nothing that we said—YOU, who treated us as alarmists when we told you of the danger of France—YOU, who would not even open the letters which were addressed to you from the departments—

YOU, who could not watch the gulf of Lyons with the whole Toulon fleet—YOU, so pusillanimous in the hour of danger, so incapable of taking a resolution, following a plan, or conceiving an idea—YOU, who had only time to hide yourselves, leaving thirty-five millions* in hard cash, for the immediate use of the usurper, so difficult was it to find half a dozen waggons,—it is YOU—YOU—who dare reproach the royalists, scattered and disarmed by YOURSELVES, for not having saved the King! Oh, you had better have held your peace, than have exposed yourselves to hear that you and your dreadful systems are the cause of all the mischief—of all the misfortune. If you had not alienated all the royalists, and advanced all the revolutionists—if you had not "cooled our friends, and heated our enemies"—the usurper could never have succeeded.

It was your revolutionary Prefects, your Buonapartist governors, who opened France to this calamity.

Did you not adroitly place major-generals all through the south, that he might not want creatures and partisans along the line of his march. Well might he say that his eagles would fly from steeple to steeple. He travelled commodiously from prefecture to prefecture,

* About 1,500,000*l*. sterling.—*Trans.*

sleeping every night (thanks to your care) at *a friend's house*;—and it is YOU who complain of the royalists! Who is there who does not know, that in all countries the civil and military bodies do all,—the unarmed crowd can do nothing? Where did the usurper meet the slightest opposition, except where, by accident, he met some of those men who were not in your blessed *revolutionary interests?*

Your agents, your clever men, overwhelmed with the favours of the crown, resisted the Royalists, and even prevented the Marseillois from marching to Marseilles. It well becomes YOU to charge upon the devoted and faithful servants of the King the results of your own weakness and cowardice.

Abandon, if you are now grown wise, a line of defence as impolitic as impudent; it proves nothing but the vices of your boasted system.

CHAPTER LXIII.

IF THERE BE NO ROYALISTS IN FRANCE, WE OUGHT TO MAKE THEM.

HAVING denied, and, I trust, disproved your major, I will now change my ground for yours, and grant you all they ask.

I then say, if even it were true that there are no royalists in France, it is the duty of the King's government to make some. Instead of *revolutionary interests*, and republican predilections, every effort ought to be strained to secure the triumph of the principles of legitimate monarchy.

Finding, by a lucky chance, a Chamber entirely and sincerely loyal, made to its hand, the Ministry should have employed it to change the bad disposition which it supposes to exist in France. And let it not be said that this was impossible: the means of a wise government are infinite. To be sure it is pleasant, after having seen all the phases of the revolutionary moon—all the various characters that all the various men have played—all the oaths of allegiance and fidelity to the first Constitution and to the last—to the Republic, to Buonaparte, to royalty, to the Government *de jure*, and to the Government *de facto*—to hear a government gravely talk of the difficulty of influencing the obstinate and inflexible character of the nation to its legitimate duty and natural allegiance.

But if we are both wrong—if the majority are, as you say, not royalists, or are, as I say, not revolutionists—if, in fact, they are indifferent or neuter—what a facility have you not of swaying them towards the principles of religion and loyalty. It is, then, it can be only from choice and taste that you embrace the system of *revolutionary interests*.

One of you has said, in his place in Parliament, that Ministers should direct the public opinion. I take you at your words—create royalists, or I impeach you for not being royalists yourselves.

CHAPTER LXIV.

THE SYSTEM APPLIED TO THE PRESENT CHAMBER OF DEPUTIES.

The greatest embarrassment of the partizans of the revolutionary doctrine—that *there are no royalists in France*—is the composition of the Chamber of Deputies.

The system of *revolutionary interests* begat the system of *no royalists;* and this again produces the doctrine, that the present Chamber does not represent the public opinion.

This is the fourth absurdity which is derived from that original blunder, that Ministers are independent of majorities; — evil makes evil.

Hear how they labour to show that the loyalty of the Chambers proves nothing.

" The opinion of the majority of the Chamber is not that of France. This Chamber was elected by surprise, and assembled during an invasion. Amidst so much confusion and danger, the Electoral Colleges made good haste to elect royalists; because, though the opinion of the colleges were against them, they thought they were about to become all-powerful. It is the minority of the Chambers which really represents the feeling of the country; and it is for that reason that Ministers act with them, choosing to obey the wishes of the nation rather than the clamours of a faction."

CHAPTER LXV.

REFUTATION.

LET me begin by observing that I find in this objection the confirmation of what I advanced a little while since, that " even if there were no royalists in France, it were easy to make them."

Observe their own statements—the Electoral Colleges are assembled in the simple expectation that the royalists are to become powerful, that the government is about to take steps in their favour ; these Colleges forthwith elect—contrary to their own wishes, conviction, and interests—royalist deputies. If this be true, I repeat that Ministers are exceedingly culpable for not making the whole nation royalists ; it can, it seems, be easily done, since so small a degree of influence has already had such wonderful effects.

But for my part, I disclaim these hypothetical arguments, strongly as they are in my favour, and I appeal to facts.

I had myself the honour of being President of the Electoral College in a city where the garrison of the Allies were separated from the army of the Loire only by a bridge. If any where there might have been expected confusion, oppression, anxiety, it was surely there. Well; there was no such thing! I saw nothing but tranquillity, confidence, hope, and the most perfect freedom of opinion: the assembly was numerous—hardly any one was absent; men of all characters and of all parties were there, even the sick caused themselves to be brought thither to exercise their franchise The result of all this was the election of four royalists; and if there had been twenty vacancies, twenty royalists would have been elected. It would have been difficult---impossible, I believe---to have procured the election of one partisan of the *revolutionary interests.*

But perhaps *my* evidence may be suspected to be tinctured by my known sentiment. But there were other Presidents who were not liable to that imputation, and yet they too had to return royalist candidates.

If, then, there was so much tranquillity and independence at Orleans, how much freer must have been the elections of the departments further removed from the convulsions of the moment.

Another proof that the Deputies spoke the sentiments of the people is the reception they met with from their constituents. I do not speak of the triumphant welcome given to some of the more remarkable members—it may be said that the spirit of party had something to say to that—but I speak of the cordiality and gratitude with which even the most obscure members of that assembly have been every where received, and only because they voted with the majority.

It has been said, indeed, that the police sent secret orders to procure for the members of its favorite minority similar triumphs—but this must be a calumny: at least there were no such triumphs.

If the departments had at first been surprised into the election of Deputies whom they did not regard, it must be admitted that they had time enough to recover themselves—to find out that the royalists were not become all-powerful, and that loyalty was not the road to favour; if then these departments were really not royalist, and if thev disapproved all that had been done during the session, they might have shewn some little symptoms of regret at their improvident choice. Not at all—they even appeared more and more satisfied with it. This is a whimsical proof of disapprobation, and the terror and surprise of these electors are strangely long-lived.

And yet what was not done to change and distract the public mind—what calumnies, what insults had not this majority to endure from the government press?

One time the Deputies were about to restore the old regime, and undo all that had been done; again, they were plotting against the royal prerogative, and preparing to oppose the King.

How could the country learn the falsehood of these reports, when the press was not free—when it was in the hands of the ministers—when beyond the barriers of Paris one had no means of explaining one's conduct, or of stating the singular position in which the most faithful servants of the crown were placed? And to crown the whole, the prorogation took place immediately after the famous report of the budget to the Chamber of Peers; and the Deputies, without an opportunity of reply or explanation, were sent home, each with articles of impeachment, as it were, in his pocket—and yet the truth was known.

Deceived, as one for ever is, in the society of Paris, where one hears and sees only his own little circle; where one's wishes pass for facts; where one's own opinions are circulated till they return in appearance the opinions of others; where flattery worships the lowest clerk as basely as the greatest minister; we heard it whispered, with a generous, though rather ostentatious pity, that " ministers would be obliged to exercise their authority to protect the Deputies, and that these poor devils would be hissed, hooted, and pelted by their constituents." Ride, si sapis!

It seems to me, that the departments are beginning to throw off the yoke of Paris.

When the Duke of Guise (surnamed Le Balafré) shewed his mother the list of towns which had acceded to the league, "My dear son," replied the Duchess of Nemours, "all that is of no consequence; if you have not Paris, you have nothing."

If the administration persist in widening the difference between Paris and the provinces, it will make a very important change in France.

CHAPTER LXVI.

COUNCILS OF THE DEPARTMENTS.

SOPHISTRY creates delusion; delusion begets detection; detection exasperates vanity: as with a losing gamester—ill success makes him more desperate.

It is so easy to say, "I beg pardon, I was wrong;" but it never happens.

The departments had received their Deputies with applause; this reception tended, to be sure, to prove that there *were royalists in France;* but the ministers had yet a resource.—The Councils of the departments were about to assemble; if these bodies should complain of the Deputies, or even treat them coolly, all were not yet lost!

The opinion of these Councils would then have been swelled into the greatest importance; we should have heard, "Well, you see how it is—I told you what would happen: there, now you have the real sentiments of France, are you at last persuaded that the Chamber does not represent the national feeling—that this feeling is altogether in unison with the *revolutionary interests?* Listen to the Council-General of the department, that is the true organ of the public voice."

Mighty fine! but what happened?

THE COUNCILS ALSO APPLAUDED THE DEPUTIES.

Then, indeed, we were told—"Oh, it is well *known* that all this was a prepared scene—a trick of cabal and party; we *know* how easy it is to procure addresses; we know how—&c."

Orders to the newspapers to quiz the triumph of the Deputies—orders to the Councils-General not to send up their addresses by a deputation: the addresses, indeed, will be received, if sent by the "post," and after they have been judiciously curtailed, and that all approbation of the Deputies has been suppressed, will appear, *by extracts*, in the Moniteur.—Finally, because the Councils had voted thanks to the Deputies—Orders that in future the Councils should vote no thanks without the express permission of the crown!!!

In order to color and excuse this last extraordinary order, a reason was assigned which is absolutely false; it was said, "that the crown alone, in all times, was the sole fountain of honor, and could alone dispense such approbation." But every body knows, that from the days of Clovis to our own, all cities, bodies, and corporations of all kinds, have exercised this right—nay, (to quote a ridiculous, but decisive example) the guns have been fired, even in Paris, in honor of the boy who has won the prize at the university.

And even if it had been true that this right had not existed in the old absolute monarchy, still it might and must belong to a constitutional monarchy. If the departments have a right to elect Deputies, they must have a right to approve or disapprove of their conduct.

What miserable shifts are these! but such is the fatal spirit of the system and of party. The best-intentioned men in the world act in direct opposition to good sense and good faith—with the most generous views, they govern, like Buonaparte, by the narrowest and most ungenerous means. But have they the power of Buonaparte?

The addresses become public; they arrive from all quarters; every body receives copies; every body sees why the ministers wished to stifle them; every body either laughs or blushes at their folly, and is more convinced than ever, that the Deputies possess the confidence, and speak the sentiments of the people.

CHAPTER LXVII.

THE OPINION OF EVEN THE MINORITY IS NOT IN FAVOR OF *REVOLUTIONARY INTERESTS.*

BUT if I grant that the minority of the Chamber does speak the general opinion of France, I will even still assert, that this opinion, fairly considered, is not in favor of *revolutionary interests.*

When the Chamber met, it was almost unanimous. It requires all the art and power of ministers to divide it. It is inconceivable how men of common sense, finding so admirable an instrument ready to their hand, and so fit for all their work, should throw it away, and labour to create and attach to themselves a *minority* with as much assiduity, as other ministers employ to gain over a *majority.*

What pains, what trouble have they not taken to be defeated—what precautions to lose this game!

First they instituted a kind of club. But the whole Chamber was so thoroughly royalist, that it was with great difficulty and only by the perpetual use of the KING'S name, that they succeeded in obtaining a few members to join it; and thus this very minority is composed of persons, who are so royalist as not to think the majority sufficiently so. This is so true, that on several occasions (as, for instance, in the discussion relative to the regicides) this minority voted with enthusiasm, and by acclamation, with the majority. Now, certainly, the punishment of the regicides was a mortal blow to *revolutionary interests.*

How then can they adduce the opinion of the minority as in favor of those interests? In fact, it is not the opinion of the minority which is of this color, but that of the ministers themselves, who endeavour to force it on the minority, which they have created.

CHAPTER LXVIII.

CONCLUSION OF THE PROOFS, THAT THE REVOLUTIONARY INTERESTS ARE NOT THOSE OF FRANCE.

LET us try the argument inversely.

If the *revolutionary interests* were all-powerful in France, every political measure would be delicate and dangerous; every attack upon them would risk the safety of the state. "See," we should hear, "see what your rashness has done; the *revolutionary interests* are menaced, and at that moment the national tranquillity is threatened; this spark will produce a devastating conflagration."

We look—we see nothing: there is no disturbance—the spark creates no conflagration. We see a few individual jacobins fall into a pit of their own digging; we see it with pleasure, and the people see it with contempt. That party has no root in the public mind, it is wholly innoxious, unless when we patronise it, and then indeed it is dangerous: as the snake which you can crush with your heel, will sting you to death if warmed in your bosom.

CHAPTER LXIX.

ROYALISTS ARE NOT TO BE MADE BY THE *REVOLUTIONARY SYSTEM*.

LET us now enter on a new field.

I have said, that you ought to make royalists if there were none "It is precisely for that purpose," say the ministers, "that we protect the *revolutionary interests*. The master-piece of our administration would be to bring over to loyalty and their duty the King's enemies. We shall conciliate all those men who can only be reproached with a little too much energy, and who will hereafter employ that same energy, in defence of the throne, which they once exerted against it."

And I, too, I have preached this doctrine; I too have advised the healing of wounds, the forgiveness of error, oblivion of the past. What tributes have I not paid to the army! I own it. I am too susceptible of the illusions of military glory; and the beat of a drum disturbs my soberer judgment. But then, what I said on this subject, before the fatal 20th of March, I can say no longer. To be too easy, too placable, is one thing; it is another to be a fool. No! one mistake is, at least, pardonable—but I should be ashamed to be *twice* duped.

You expect to make royalists the men who have already ruined you ;—by what acts ? What can you now do for them that was not done before ? They filled all places ; they were gorged with wealth ; they were covered with honors. Some regicides a monthly pension of a thousand crowns, only for having cut off the King's head. Can you be *more* liberal than this ?

The * *hundred days* have festered the wound ; they have added, to the old hatred, the new shame of having committed a second treachery, and the new mortification of having failed.

Thus, legitimacy is become more odious than ever to such men ; their feelings can be assuaged only by its destruction.

I repeat it—to hope, after what passed on the 20th of March, to hope to conciliate the revolutionists ;—to place power in the hands of the natural enemies of royalty ;—to pursue the ridiculous project of amalgamation and fusion ; —to believe that vanity can be won by patronage, or passions controlled by interest ;— in short, to fall again into all the faults for which we have received so recent and so severe a chastisement,—is a degree of madness that almost makes me fear that Providence has pronounced some fatal sentence upon my unhappy country.

* Of the second usurpation.—*Trans.*

CHAPTER LXX.

OF "EPURATIONS" IN GENERAL.

This leads to the consideration of that species of moral revision of the composition of public bodies, and the consequent exclusion of improper characters, which in French we call *epurations* *

Before the commencement of the session, the Electoral Colleges had demanded the *epuration* of the magistracy, and other public bodies. At the opening of the session, the two Chambers repeated this demand; the ministers evaded it by replying that they would closely watch their agents, and that they made themselves responsible for all events.

But first let me ask what is this responsibility of ministers?

The law which is to define it, is not yet enacted. This responsibility is a mere bugbear. It looks tremendous through the haze —when it comes near, it is nothing.

The first cabinet was undoubtedly devoted

* The nearest English word is *purification*, but it does not fully convey the meaning of epuration.—*Trans.*

to the King; yet was it able to prevent the treachery of its clerks and officers? In the crowd of cases in which a minister must see with the eyes and hear with the ears of his assistants and subordinates, who can insure him from misrepresentations? If, for example, all the underlings of an extensive department calumniate the true friends of the King, can the minister avoid taking the colour of their eternal reports?

Whenever we use this word *epuration* *, they cry out, " You mean *vengeance*, you mean *re-action*."

I have already said that justice is not vengeance,—that oblivion is not re-action,—that no man ought to be persecuted—but that public stations should not be filled by the King's enemies. Why is there such a bustle with a certain class of men at the very sound of the word *justice*? It is because they feel *that* to be the rub. Ay, if once we were to come to *justice*, it is all over with those who, even now, have not given up their guilty hopes. What do they care about liberty or the Charter, words so frequently in their lips? Nothing. They care for themselves, their places, and their power; secure these to them, and you may do as you will with the rest of France.

When ministers were pressed on this subject

by the public voice, they adopted a tone of temporising policy. They said, "Let us alone, we shall make the necessary revision; but we shall do it quietly and by degrees, that we may not all at once disorganize the departments, and stop the course of public business."

This answer might satisfy a minister, but it would not have satisfied a statesman. Is there any possible case, in which it is not better to have an *inexperienced* agent, than a *treacherous* one?

"But if you make so many changes, you will create a host of enemies to the government."

But are these enemies more formidable out of doors than in the heart of your government? The influence of a placeman, however small his place, is yet infinitely greater than the influence of the same man as a private indi vidual.

Besides, I repeat, you will not succeed with these men; you do not conciliate them; your caresses appear to them hypocrisy; they know that you cannot love them; they flatter and laugh in their sleeve at your system of *fusion*, because they know that it leads to your ruin; and by and by, to prove your incapability, and to justify some new revolution, they will adduce in evidence against you, vour confidence and vourf avours.

Let us suppose that these public servants do not give way to their political hostility:—How can you prevent them from being warped by feelings more excusable, but not less dangerous? In your present system of government, the virtues of a man are to be dreaded as well as his vices; he must stifle, if he does his duty, the voice of nature and the best sentiments of the heart. He must arrest his friend; he must prosecute his benefactor:—you place him between his duties and his feelings, and his fidelity is calculated upon his ingratitude.

CHAPTER LXXI.

PARTIAL "EPURATIONS" UNJUST.

After all, when the Ministers had once adopted the system of revolutionary interests, the rejection of that of *epuration* was a necessary consequence; but then, having taken this course, they should pursue it frankly and honestly. They have not done so. Of a bad road, they have selected the worst rut to drive in. They made partial *epurations;* and converted what ought to have been a great act of justice into a flagrant injustice.

There is a natural sense of equity in mankind, which prevents their complaining of a general measure impartially applied; but partial measures, which have the appearance of caprice, disgust every body.

How have these partial *epurations* operated? One man has lost his place or his pension for having signed Buonaparte's *additional act;* another retains both, who had signed the same instrument five or six different times, in five or six different characters.

This man accepted a place during the *hundred days*, and is now dismissed from it; another did the same, and still enjoys his office.

A public functionary continued to hold under Buonaparte a high station, which he had originally received from the King—he is degraded and punished: his neighbour had solicited the usurper for the same employment, and had not obtained it;—despised by Buonaparte, he now enjoys the internal satisfaction of a pure conscience, and the external rewards of fidelity, which he has received from the legitimate government!

Fédérés have been decorated with the royal order*; and a magistrate of an obscure tribunal, who had the weakness to take some †miserable oath, suffers all the severity of *epuration*—he is dismissed.

* We presume the decoration of the lys is meant.

† We hardly can reconcile this expression with M. de Chateaubriand's known sentiments, both in religion and politics: he surely cannot mean to treat as a slight offence, perjury and treason united: a thousand ignorant rabble fédérés are surely not altogether so guilty as one magistrate, who uses his better education and higher station only to betray the King and insult heaven. And what does M. de Chateaubriand mean by *miserable* oath? Are there degrees in oaths? Must a splendid oath be kept, and may an obscure one be broken? From the context, I may say, of M. de Chateaubriand's life, and from his express declaration in subsequent chapters of this work, it is evident that this is a hasty expression *quam incuria fudit*, but it should be corrected.—*Trans.*

But as every thing in civil life, as in nature, must be counterbalanced and compensated, we have seen " en revanche" Royalists—judges, magistrates, and citizens,—who, during the *hundred days*, had conducted themselves with fidelity and firmness, turned out of their places, which were immediately given to the partisans of the Usurper; — wonderful impartiality! Again: when Ministers have been forced by public opinion to turn out a Revolutionist, have they not removed him from one place, only to put him into a better?

It happened one day that a man, of whom I knew nothing, but who, I found, had been turned out in consequence of those partial *epurations*, came to ask me some favour; he had the simplicity to tell me, that a certain Minister had promised to replace him in his office as soon as *that damned Chamber* should be dissolved. He meant the Deputies.

I admired the wisdom of Providence, and thanked Heaven, that this worthy person should have, of all men in the world, addressed himself to *me*.

These *epurations* produce another evil; they create parties in the provinces, they encourage petty vengeances, secret jealousies, and denunciations. Any one who happens to cast a longing eye on his neighbour's place, will not fail to recollect all his neighbours' faults, or to invent a few for him.

If Ministers had at first, struck a great blow—if there had been an enlarged and just *epuration*, all would have been settled at once, and the public vengeance would have been satisfied.

Now they complain of denunciations, and they are right;—but whose fault is it? do they not flow from their own half measures? ought not a Minister to know his own mind? It would have been much better to have said at once, there shall be no revision, no épuration, and to have adhered fairly to that resolution, than to waver between that resolution and its opposite—to be alike unable to adopt the one, or to persevere in the other.

CHAPTER LXXII.

THE ALLEGED INCAPACITY OF THE ROYALISTS, —THE ALLEGED ABILITY OF THEIR ADVERSARIES.

It is pretended (and this is the last of these pretences to which I have to reply), it is pretended, that the Royalists are incapable; and that there is no talent in France except in the school of Bonaparte and the Revolution.

Is any proof of this adduced? No; the thing is considered as demonstrated, "we wish" say the Ministers, "that we had a great many Royalists, but they should be such as we can employ: as there are none, we are obliged to adopt the servants of Bonaparte, because they alone know how to do business."

Thus the circle of their argument is complete—the Royalists have no talent,—therefore, we cannot employ them—therefore, we cannot turn out the Bonapartists—therefore, we must favour *Revolutionary interests.*

I beg to interpose one question, Have those who have governed France since the restoration been Royalists?

If you say Yes; then indeed I agree with

you that your assertion is proved, and that the Royalists are fools. They have committed enormous errors.

But then there is this little consolation; if *incapacity* is the distinctive mark of a Royalist it must be allowed that certain Ministers have been grossly calumniated when it has been said that they were not attached to the King; for my part, I hold them to have been, *in this view of the case*, as liege subjects as ever lived in this realm, since the days of good King Dagobert down to the present time.

But if you answer in the negative; and if the Ministers since the restoration have *not* been Royalists; then I ask, where is your boasted ability, where the triumphant talents of those men of the Revolution?

Look at what they have done; could Royalists have done worse?

It is really miraculous that men who fall with the slightest touch—who cannot make a step without stumbling—who let Bonaparte march to Paris, and who left France and the King to shift for themselves as well as they could—it is miraculous I say, that these folks should dare to talk of their own talents, and to sneer at the imbecility of the King's friends.

You who have failed—so lamentably, so disasterously failed—should at least not claim such a prodigious superiority, till the Royalists have been tried.

Make the experiment: see what they can do. If they are more incapable, if they are more ridiculous than you, turn them out; you will resume the reins and your systems will be justified.

One thing however we may affirm;—if, before the 20th March, the Government and all its agents had been composed of Royalists, they might not, perhaps, have been able to prevent the return of Bonaparte, but at least they would neither have betrayed the King, nor served the Usurper. Eighty-four Prefects,—dolts if you will, but obstinately bent on opposing Bonaparte—might have given him some little trouble.

There are cases in which fidelity is talent, as good old La Fontaine's instinct was genius.

CHAPTER LXXIII.

FALSEHOOD AND DANGER OF THE OPINION THAT ABILITY IS CONFINED TO MEN OF THE REVOLUTION.

The opinion that there is no talent in France except in the men of the Revolution, is alike false and dangerous, as we have already sadly experienced. My noble friend, M. de Bonald, said, that Buonaparte could create Ministers, but was unable to form Statesmen:—a just observation; of which the following is a commentary.

What, under a despot, is a Minister? He is a man who receives an order which, whether just or unjust, he executes; who has no opinion of his own, "who admits no force in argument, "and employs no argument but force."

Remove such a Minister to a constitutional monarchy—oblige him to think for himself—to select a line of conduct—to find the means of carrying the measures of the Government, of conciliating interests, and reconciling opinions, without offending the law—and you will see this man whom you looked upon as a giant, dwindle to a dwarf. All his mysteries, his calculations, all his "positive results," all his statistical abstracts will fail him at once. It will no longer be of any use to him to know how many head of cattle are to be found in one department, or how much pulse, poultry, and eggs, is furnished by another. Smith and Malthus will be of no avail to him. Whenever moral and political combinations become necessary, this *square*-headed Statesman will blunder in every thing, and the great Minister will be discovered to be a great fool.

I have seen these boasted idols of despotic administration, disconcerted, astonished, and, as it were, lost, in a free Government. Unacquainted with religion and justice—the natural means of such a Government—they always attempt to apply physical force to the moral system of things; less fitted for that system than the lowest of the Royalists, they find themselves stopped in their progress by invisible boundaries, and they struggle with a power unknown and incomprehensible to them.

Hence their bad laws, their false systems, their opposition to all true principles. A slave cannot all at once comprehend independence;—an infidel is not at ease near the altar. Do not imagine that the men of the Revolution have still preserved their fatal and peculiar talent. The *faculty for evil* which they possessed, has become useless, under a moral and regular Government! They are, as it were, dead in the midst of a new world which rises around them; and they wander among us like the empty shadows, and carry about the lifeless bodies of their former selves.

CHAPTER LXXIV.

THE SYSTEM OF REVOLUTIONARY INTERESTS, BY TENDING TO THE OVERTHROW OF THE CHARTER, THREATENS THE DESTRUCTION OF THE LEGITIMATE MONARCHY.

I THINK I have demonstrated that the system of *Revolutionary interests* rests entirely on erroneous principles; that those who follow it are obliged to take refuge in the most unconstitutional heresies; that the measures adopted in consequence of that system have necessarily created the Opposition—the inevitable result of the false position in which the ministers have placed themselves.

But this is not all—hitherto I have only considered the futility of the system. I shall now point out its danger.

It leads in the first place indirectly to the subversion of the Charter; for if we always have, as it is to be hoped we shall, Deputies possessing courage and independence, they will continue to resist revolutionary maxims; and to get rid of such troublesome opponents, it will be found convenient to violate the Constitution. Indeed what have the Ministeralists not said of the Charter, even in their places in the Chamber! In what strange modes do they explain and interpret it! and to what would they not reduce it, if it were in their power! And yet, to hear them, it is *we* who are not constitutional.—It is *I*, perhaps of all men, who am an enemy to the Charter.

If the system of *Revolutionary interests* should bring about the destruction of nothing else than the Charter, the best work of the King, it would be, I think, an evil of sufficient magnitude; but I maintain that the overthrow of legitimate monarchy would immediately and inevitably follow.

It is necessary to speak out; the period of forbearance is gone by. God grant that I may prove to be a false prophet! May my alarms have no other source than excess of love for my King and his family! But though I draw upon myself party fury, and personal hatred, I shall still have courage to tell the whole truth. If I be deceived, if there be in reality no danger, my words will be scattered by the winds; if on the contrary, conspiracy and danger exist, I may be the means of opening the eyes of honest men. A plot discovered is half defeated: unmask factions and you deprive them of power.

CHAPTER LXXV.

THERE EXISTS A CONSPIRACY AGAINST LEGITIMATE MONARCHY.

I affirm then. that an actual conspiracy is formed against legitimate Monarchy.

I do not say that this conspiracy resembles an ordinary conspiracy ;—that it is the result of the machinations of a certain number of traitors ready to strike a sudden blow, to attempt a forcible deposition or assassination, although I must say it is not unattended by dangers even of *that* description :—I only say that there exists as it were a conspiracy of the *moral* interests of the Revolution, a natural association of all those whose consciences reproach them with any crime or baseness ; in a word, a conspiracy of illegitimacies of all sorts against every thing that is legitimate.

I say that this conspiracy operates every where, and at all times ; that it instinctively opposes all that tends to consolidate the throne, to re-establish the principles of religion, morality, justice, and honour. The hour of its success I cannot foresee ; different causes may hasten or retard it, but it considers itself sure of success. In the meanwhile it works to bring about that success, and derives its chief means of action from the *system of Revolutionary interests !*

CHAPTER LXXVI.

THE SECRET PURPOSE CONCEALED BEHIND THE SYSTEM OF REVOLUTIONARY INTERESTS.

THE system which it is pretended must be followed, for the safety of the Throne, and the tranquillity of the State, conceals within itself the secret purpose for which it has been adopted, and to the triumph of which it is directed.

It is laid down as a maxim by a certain party, that a revolution such as ours, can be terminated only by a change of dynasty. Others who are more moderate say, by a change in the order of succession : I shall refrain from entering into the detail of these criminal and treasonable propositions.

Who is to be placed on the throne instead of the Bourbons ? On this point opinions are divided, but they are agreed on the necessity of deposing the legitimate family. The Stuarts are the example cited. History tempts them ;— had it not been for the execution of Charles I, we should not deplore that of Louis XVI ; Wretched imitators ! you did not even invent the crime.

How shall I prove that this horrible doctrine is mysteriously hidden under the system of *Revolutionary interests?*

I need only cast a glance on the pamphlets and journals of the *hundred days*.

I have since read, and others have likewise read, publications which leave nothing doubtful, not even the name. Amidst the gaiety of the table, or in the heat of discussion, which is another sort of intoxication, candour avows and levity betrays their secret thoughts. But if I wanted direct proofs, I need only cast my eyes on *what is passing around* me: whenever one sees a uniform plan, and regular parts connected and corresponding with each other, it is evident that such regularity could not have been the effect of chance: a consequence leads me to look for a principle: and through the nature of the effect I arrive at the character of the cause.

Let us observe the object, and follow the progress of this conspiracy.

CHAPTER LXXVII.

OBJECT AND PROGRESS OF THE CONSPIRACY.—ITS FIRST EFFORTS ARE DIRECTED AGAINST THE ROYAL FAMILY.

The chief object of that which I term the conspiracy of the moral interests of the Revolution, is to change the dynasty; its secondary object is to impose on the new Sovereign the conditions to which it endeavoured to subject the King at St. Dennis: namely, to adopt the tri-coloured cockade, to acknowledge himself to be King by the grace of the People, to re-embody the army of the Loire, and recall the representatives of Bonaparte, if they should happen to be alive at the period. The present existence of this project, which has never been abandoned, will be rendered completely evident by the observation of facts which stare us in the face.

It is agreed in the first place to speak of the King in the same manner as he is spoken of by the Royalists themselves; to acknowledge that which no one can deny, his eminent virtues and superior knowledge.—The King—so insulted during the *hundred days*—has become all at once an object of praise to those who basely betrayed him, and are ready to betray him again.

But these marks of admiration and love are merely clokes for the attack directed against the rest of the Royal Family. The *ambition* of the Princes,—who have on all occasions shewn themselves the most faithful and obedient of subjects,—is spoken of with an affectation of fear. A Constitutional Government, with *different centres of power*, is declared to be impossible. The Princes must therefore be removed from the Council; the party even go so far as to pretend that there are inconveniencies in allowing the King's brother to hold the chief command of the National Guards of the kingdom, and endeavours are made to restrain and shackle his authority.

It has been proposed to make the Duke of Angoulême Patron of the University of Paris, and thus to render him, as it were, the Prince of our Youth.—This is a simple and effective mode of attaching the rising generations to a family scarcely known to them. Youth is susceptible of devotion and enthusiasm. Nothing could be more politic than to give them as guardian, the Prince who is destined to become their

Sovereign. But will this measure be adopted?—I dare not hope that it will.

The reason of this conduct is easily discovered. The faction—which acts under loyal and faithful Ministers, who do not perceive the precipice to which they are pushed—wishes to change dynasty. It it therefore hostile to every thing capable of connecting France with her legitimate magistrates. It fears that the Royal Family will strike its roots too deeply. It tries to insulate and separate that family from the Crown. Its partizans have the audacity to hint, nay, to say, to say openly, that affairs may go on in the present way in France for the King's life, but that after his death we shall have another revolution. Thus the people are habituated to regard the present order of things as transitory. That which is not believed to be durable, is the more easily overthrown.

While they endeavour on one hand to divest the heirs of the Crown of all power, they, on the other, attempt, thank God in vain, to deprive them of the respect and veneration of the people. Their virtues are calumniated. The foreign journals are *principally* charged with this part of the attack; but we have seen in our own journals, things alike indecent and absurd? What is meant by publishing with so much parade the intrigues of a few wretched underlings? If they compromise none but the men mentioned, do they deserve to occupy the attention of Europe? and if illustrious names are in any way connected, why this singular desire to make them known? Those who are averse to the liberty of the press, will at least confess, that to these embarrassing questions that liberty would furnish a reply, if not satisfactory, at least unanswerable; but they who controul the press must be responsible for it.

Let us distinguish between real and false Royalists: the former are those who never separate the King from the Royal Family, who confound them together in the same feeling of devotion and love, who joyfully obey the sceptre of the one, and do not fear the influence of the other;—the latter are those who, whilst they pretend to idolize the Monarch, declaim against the Princes of his blood,—would plant the lily in a desert, and would tear away all the shoots which surround the royal stem.

In ordinary and tranquil times, when the authority of the Crown has not been shaken by Revolution, considerations may arise as to the part which the Princes of the blood should be permitted to take in the Government; but after all our misfortunes, after so many years of usurpation, he who does not feel the necessity of multiplying the bonds of union between the French people and the Royal Family, of attaching the nation, and all its ranks and interests to the descendants of Saint Louis; he who affects to dread the heirs, more than the enemies of the throne, is a man whose mind is declining quietly into folly, or rapidly into treason.

CHAPTER LXXVIII.

THE CONSPIRACY EMPLOYS THE SYSTEM OF REVOLUTIONARY INTERESTS TO INTRODUCE ITS AGENTS INTO ALL PLACES OF TRUST.

To attack by all sorts of means the Royal Family—to be constantly on the look out for a misfortune which every good Frenchman would redeem with his own life, and which he hopes never to see—to wish for the eternal exile of the Princes, as a consequence of that misfortune —and to sleep and wake on these frightful hopes; is what the hostile sect first teaches to the initiated.

The greatest efforts are next made to extend and propagate the system of *Revolutionary interests*. To the timid that system is exhibited as a port of safety; to fools as a conception of genius; and to dupes as the means of consolidating Royalty.

By the complete establishment of this system the Revolutionists hope that they will, when the crisis arrives, have all the Offices of Government in their possession. All the authorities being then in the same interest, the change will be effected—as on the 20th of March—

by a common understanding, without resistance, and without striking a blow.

What does it cost these men to deny their masters? Nothing. Did they not desert Buonaparte himself? Within the space of a few months they alternately assumed, abandoned, and resumed, the white, and the tri-coloured cockade. The arrival of a Courier at once changed their hearts and the colour of their riband. Only hear with what delightful simplicity they speak of their signature to the Additional Act. "They did no harm; they are innocent as "Abel." They only wrote abominable calumnies against the Bourbons; only insulted them in a thousand Proclamations: but what of that—they now *levée* the Princes with these Proclamations in their pockets. They speak, without even a wry face, of legitimate Monarchy, of loyalty, of devotion, of honour. You would imagine they came from the forests of La Vendee, and yet they are hot from the Champ-de-Mai.

They are in the right, however; for every time that they violate the faith they have sworn, they obtain a new office. The age of an old deer is reckoned by the branches of his horns, these men's places may be counted by their oaths.

In vain then do you hope they will remain

attached to you, when all the power of the Monarchy shall be confided to them. They look for places now, as they did before the 20th of March, only to be the better able to ruin you. Already do they boast their success, their hopes are grown insolent, and they cannot restrain their joy at the growing prosperity of *Revolutionary interests.*

"We betrayed you," say they, "but it was because you gave us only three-fourths of the places. Give us *all*, and you will see how faithful we shall be." Aye, encrease the dose and you will find that the poison, instead of killing, will cure you! And yet there are pretended Royalists who maintain this absurdity! All that can be said is, that if they once were Royalists, they are Royalists no longer.

CHAPTER LXXIX.

CONTINUATION OF THE SAME SUBJECT.

The faction insists upon having all the places, all the offices,—and generally succeeds in obtaining them. The permanence *(Inamovabilitè)* of the Judges was the subject of their warm opposition. But worthy Jacobins in permanent offices are most useful men,—they keep the sacred fire alive, and extend a helping hand to their less fortunate brethren.

In the administration of the Finances, and the offices depending upon it, the *Revolutionary interests* are maintained with vigour.—A Clerk who had fled returns, perhaps promoted, to the town where he was but too well known during the *hundred days*. What do people think on seeing this man? Why, that he was in the right when he foretold to them the events of the 20th of March, and that he is right again when he promises a similar occurrence, by the phrase :—*When* THE OTHER *comes back*.

In the Home department, the *Revolutionary interests* were at first somewhat depressed. Their Camp was alarmed: the Royalist impulse frightened them: but the party speedily collected its spirits and its forces. Obstacles were soon thrown in the way of appointments and dismissals of too royalist a colour, by submitting all appointments and dismissals to the examination of the council of Ministers: so that the Minister of Justice should have the power of creating a General, and the Minister of War a Judge.

Had this singular restriction been imposed equally on all the Ministers, one might have been content with smiling at it; but it was applied only to such Ministers as were suspected of Royalism. Those who are known to have openly supported the system of *Revolutionary interests*, have the privilege of nominating suspected men, and of removing all such as are notoriously loyal.

But these arrangements did not sufficiently satisfy the party. The Royalist Minister must be overthrown: that accomplished, their hopes were re-animated and confirmed. They now expected the Royalists would be driven from every inch of ground which they had gained in this branch of the administration. The National Guard was attacked. Prefects suspected of too much loyalty have been already dismissed; others are threatened. The party will be particularly careful to remove the friends of the throne, and should it be so fortunate as to obtain the dissolution of the Chamber of Deputies, it would find it more easy to direct and influence the new elections.

CHAPTER LXXX.

WAR.

Every Minister, at all remarkable for loyalty, finds great difficulty in maintaining himself; but the Minister of War is particularly disliked; they never can forgive his generous devotion, and still less his success, in forming an excellent gendarmerie, and a loyal army. These works, which would defeat all their plans, must be undone,—and as the Minister could not be at once overthrown, it was necessary to render him unpopular with the Royalist party; to ask him for *pledges*, to force upon him some vexatious dismissal, or some unfortunate choice. At the same time efforts were made to revive the army of the Loire. We may admire the courage of that army, but let us take care how we restore to it a power which it has so grossly abused. The army of Charles VII. likewise retired to the banks of the Loire; but La Hire and Dunois, still fought for the Lily, and Jeanne d'Arc in spite of the King, saved Orleans for him and for France.

CHAPTER LXXXI.

THE FACTION PERSECUTES THE ROYALISTS.

The Faction seizes on every post, retreats slowly when it is pressed, advances with rapidity when it observes the least opening, and profits by our faults as much as by its own victories.

Insinuating and confident, the language of these men is moderation, oblivion of the past, and forgiveness of injuries,—but their thoughts and their actions are all hatred and violence. Whilst they support their friends, raise them to power, and establish them in places, in order to make use of them in the critical moment,—they discourage, insult, and persecute the Royalists that they may not, at the same moment, stand in their way.

They have invented a new jargon too in order to advance their object. At the commencement of the Revolution they spoke of the *Aristocrats*, they now talk of the *Ultra-Royalists*. The foreign journals in their pay or their interests call us simply *Ultras*. *We* are then the *Ultras; we*, alas, the unhappy heirs of those Aristocrats whose ashes repose in the promiscuous graves of * Picpus and the *Madeleine.* By means of the Police, the Faction governs the public papers, and laughs with presumptuous security at those who are not permitted to defend themselves. The great watch-word is, *one must not be more Royalist than the King.* This phrase is not quite new; it was invented under Louis XVI. to tie the hands of the loyal, and to leave nothing free but the arm of the executioner.

Should the Royalists endeavour to collect, to recover, to fortify themselves against the coalitions of their enemies, they are accused of sedition. Grave personages are not ashamed to advance the abominable maxim,—that it is as necessary to proscribe a good principle which may have bad results, as to proscribe the most perverse doctrine:—alas then, for virtue—for its undertakings in this world almost always turn to its ruin! a Royalist is assimilated to a Jacobin; and, by an equity well worthy of the age, justice consists in balancing the scale equally between vice and innocence, between infamy and honour, between treason and fidelity.

* The bodies of the victims beheaded by the guillotine, which stood on the east side of Paris, were buried, or rather thrown into pits at Picpus; those who suffered in the Place Louis XV., were interred at the Madeleine. Trans.

CHAPTER LXXXII.

CONCLUSION OF THE FOREGOING.

DEVOTION to our duties is the eternal object of the ridicule of a class of men who would certainly care very little for the punishment inflicted by the ancient Germans on infamy—buried in mud, they would be in their own element. The journey to Ghent is nick-named the *Sentimental Journey*. This excellent joke was made by some clerks, who—loyal to their places,—served *faithfully* before, during, and since, *the hundred days*;—by some of those honest pensioners of his Majesty, who applauded with all their hearts the sentimental traveller of Elba, and who now expect his second advent from St. Helena!

Ask a favour for a soldier of the army of Condé from these gentlemen? "No," they reply, "give "us the men who have fired balls in the teeth of "allies." Now, for my part, I should like just as well those who fired balls in the teeth of the Bonapartists.

They place on the same level, Laroche Jaquelein, who fell exclaiming *Vive le Roi* on the field bathed with the blood of his illustrious brother, and some officer who died at Waterloo, blaspheming the name of the Bourbons. The cross of honour is given to the soldier who fought in that battle against the King; and the loyal volunteer who abandoned all to follow his Majesty, has not even the little riband which was promised at Alost, as the reward of his affecting fidelity.

Again: the decrees of Bonaparte, dated from the Thuilleries in May, 1815, are carefully executed, while the *ordonnances* of the King, signed at Ghent in the same month are wholly disregarded. The half-pay officer who is a member of the Legion of Honour is paid—and it is very right—but the knight of St. Louis, bent down by old age, and by adversity abroad, and more severe adversity at home,—starves upon alms: too happy if he obtain a miserable great coat to cover his nakedness, and an order of admission into the hospital, where the *Filles de la Charité*, may dress those old wounds, which are despised or forgotten like the old monarchy.

Finally, it is a folly, an error, a crime! not to have served Bonaparte. If you wish to do a young man a service, take care not to say that he saved himself from the Conscription by forfeiting half his fortune;—that he has suffered exile, persecution, and imprisonment, to avoid lending assistance to the Usurper;—that he never took any of his oaths, or accepted any of his places;—that he preserved pure and unstained his loyalty to the King, whom, at the hazard of eternal exile, he followed in his last misfortune:—these are all sufficient motives for his exclusion. "He has not served," you will be answered coldly; "he knows nothing."

Is honour nothing?

"Nonsense! the present age knows better than that!"

But, to console yourself for this refusal, propose some man who has accepted all Bonaparte would give from the high dignity of train-bearer, down to the humbler office of Imperial scullion. You have only to say; what would you have? Choose—the magistracy, the ministry, or the army. A hundred witnesses will depose in favour of your client. They will attest that they have seen him keeping watch in the Imperial anti-chambers, with extraordinary courage. He only asks a decoration; to be sure he ought to have one. Quick, let us knight him; hang to his button-hole the Cross of St. Louis.—Don't be afraid.—He is a cautious man and at a proper opportunity will prudently put it in his pocket.

O for such a man I admit it was easy to find a place; *he* was spotless: *he* had committed no offence: but you will hesitate to present this other.—*He*, during the *hundred days*, trampled,

I regret to say, the Cross of St. Louis under his feet—"Poo, is that all? a trifle; merely excess of energy: that fiery character is like generous wine, which time will mellow."

A man has during the *hundred days* been a historian of the Charnel-houses of the Police. —"Give him a pension: talents ought to be encouraged."

Another repaired to Ghent, at the risk of his life, to offer to the King money and soldiers. He solicits a small place in his village.—"A place to *him*, to an ultra!—by no means.—Give it to the Custom-House Officer who fired at him as he was passing the frontier."

You have not succeeded in obtaining the appointment of that Judge:—But do you know why?—"it was promised to an apostate Priest?"

A Prefect had prevaricated: the report of his crime was ready to present; but it is stopped—Why?—"Do you not see that such a report "would prevent us from employing him again."

Where are your Certificates? is a question put to the honest Royalist humbly soliciting the lowest place. He had suffered during twenty-five years for the King—lost his family, his fortune, health, every thing.—He has the recommendation of the Princes, of that *Princess* perhaps, whose slightest word is an oracle to all who acknowledge the influence of virtue, of heroism, and of misfortune. These recommendations, alas! are quite insufficient—worse than nothing.

A Bonapartist arrives; countenances unbend; his papers *were in the office of the Police;* but he lost them when M. Fouché was dismissed.—"That is unlucky, but we will take "your word; here, my good friend, here is "your appointment."

According to the system of *Revolutionary interests*, a man of the *hundred days* cannot be too speedily employed: too soon sent, reeking with his new treason, to infect the Palace of our Kings, as Messalina brought into that of the Cæsars the stain of her *imperial prostitutions*.

CHAPTER LXXXIII.

THE OBJECT OF PERSECUTING THE ROYALISTS.

This sort of tactics has for its object to weary out the friends of the Throne, and to deprive the Crown of its last partizans. It is intended to drive them to despair, and imprudence, of which due advantage will be taken against them, and against the monarchy. It is hoped that they may, at least, do what they have always done, and what has always ruined them—retire and submit.

Since the commencement of the Revolution, it has been the fate of the Royalists to be robbed and ridiculed. Frequent care is taken to remind them that they have nothing, that they shall have nothing, that they must expect nothing. France indeed is opened to them, but over the gate is written, as on that of Danté's hell—

"Abandon hope, all you that enter here."

If they offer all that remains to them—their arms and their services,—they are rejected. The very name of Royalist seems a proof of incapacity, a sentence to sufferings and misery.

The partisans of the system of *Revolutionary interests* are supported by the preachers of ingratitude. "The Royalists," say they, "are "not dangerous. It is useless to trouble "ourselves about their fate. If we should "want them we can always find them again."

And you do not fear that you may irretrieveably disgust by such insulting language, or weary out by oppression and poverty, those men of whom you have so high an opinion? What admirable men must these be, whom in your prosperity you repulse, but whose virtues you reserve for your days of misfortune!

You do right! they will *not* be disgusted or wearied; they will consummate their sacrifice; their patience, like their love for their King, is indefatigable and inexhaustible.

CHAPTER LXXXIV.

THE FACTION PERSECUTES RELIGION.

The Royalists would defend the King, they must therefore be removed:—the Altar would support the Throne, its restoration must therefore be prevented. The system of *Revolutionary interests* is every where incompatible with Religion; and the most powerful efforts of the party are directed against it, because it is the key-stone of legitimate Government.

At first they endeavoured to excite a civil war in the south, with a view of throwing the odium on the Catholics. All the Laws proposed by the Chambers have been rendered abortive: not one of their resolutions on the subject of religion has risen from the grave of the Minister's portfolio, to which they were consigned. This gives a double advantage to the *Revolutionary interests*;—the apostate continues to receive his pension, while the parish priest is dying of hunger.

Thus almost nothing has been done since the restoration of *the eldest son of the Church* to heal its wounds, or alleviate its degradation: and yet what does not our country owe to the Catholic religion!

The first Apostle of the French said to the first King of the French, at his coronation,— "Sicamber, adore what thou hast despised; "burn what thou hast adored." The last Apostle of the French said to the last King of the French, at his execution—"Son of St. Louis, "ascend to heaven." It is in the sentiments excited by these two addresses, that the history of the Most Christian Kings should be meditated, and that the genius of the Monarchy of St. Louis is to be sought.

The propositions favourable to the Clergy were not adopted, but the law of the 23d of September was. It was well known indeed to be a bad measure of finance, but then it was a capital revolutionary stroke. Ten millions of francs per annum (about 450,000*l.* sterling), restored to the Church, it was plain would not overload the Clergy with riches, but it would be an act of piety and justice; and justice and piety are just what we do not want, for they might counteract our system of *Revolutionary interests*.

Twenty-five years hence there will remain no priests in France, except a few wretched old men, who will show strangers where altars and temples once stood. The party calculates very skilfully; and to prevent the renewal of the Clergy, defeats every measure for supplying them with the means of an honourable existence. They know that pensions, penurious and precarious, subject to every kind of financial interruption, and to every political change, do not offer advantages sufficient to induce families to devote their children to the ecclesiastical state. Parents will not consign their children to poverty and contempt.

The game is then sure, if played with perseverance: and it will. I know not whether patience belongs to hell, as well as to heaven, on account of its eternity, but I am sure that in this world it is given to the wicked as well as the good. The physical and material destruction of religion is inevitable in France, if the secret enemies of the State—who are, a little more openly, those of the Church—should, sometimes under one pretext, sometimes under another, succeed in holding the Clergy in the state of humiliation to which they are at present reduced.

Religion, surrounded by her massacred children on the very field of battle where she fell in defence of the throne of St. Louis, still extends her feeble arms to avert the blows aimed at the King; but her assassins are vigilant, and whenever she makes an effort to rise, an arm is ready to strike her down again.

A venerable Prelate was intrusted with the direction of religious affairs; the distribution of the bread of the Martyrs was no longer entrusted to those who had kneaded it with tares, and who even did not give full measure of that bitter bread. The Revolutionists could not tolerate such an innovation in their privileges. A Minister of honourable character, and who lamented the hard incapacity of his situation, was compelled to dismiss the Prelate, and bring things back to a worse state even than they were under Buonaparte. The Clergy is replaced under the uncontrolled authority of Laymen, and religion is subjected to the secular superintendance of the Apostles of Philosophy and the Revolution.

When a poor Priest wants the month's salary which is due to him, he must present a certificate of character to the Mayor of the place in which he resides. The Mayor writes to the Sub-Prefect; who, in his turn, addresses himself to the Prefect; whose prudence induces him to refer it to the Chief Clerk in the ecclesiastical branch of the Home Department: the Chief Clerk may think it necessary to speak to the Minister, and at last this great affair being maturely examined, *eight shillings and elevenpence** are munificently paid down to the man, who consoles the afflicted, shares his mite with the poor, comforts the sick, exhorts the dying, buries the dead, and prays for his enemies, for France, and for the King!

Some ecclesiastical property had been alienated, but the contracts had not been perfected; this was discovered, and it was feared the holders might be induced to restore it to the Church. Presto—The property was instantly seized to the use of the public.

But it is not sufficient to deprive the priest of the means of living, he must also be degraded in the eyes of the people. What had never been seen under the reign of the Atheists was thought a pleasant exhibition under the reign of the Most Christian King. A priest was cited like a criminal to appear before the Court of Correctional Police. He came, poor man, in his cassock and band, and immediately found himself thrown into the dock among prostitutes and thieves. The people were struck with astonishment, and the bench, seeing their emotion, ordered the court to be cleared and the cause was heard in secret.

This hatred of religion is the distinctive character of those who have caused our misfor-

* Twelve livres ten sous!!!

tunes, and still meditate our ruin. They detest Religion because they have persecuted it, because its eternal wisdom and divine morality are in opposition with their vain wisdom and the corruption of their hearts. They never will, never can, be reconciled with it. If any among them were to shew some transient pity for an unhappy clergyman they would exclaim against such degeneracy, and believe that such a prodigy menaced their whole party with some great misfortune. When the morals of Rome were yet pure, that city was filled with consternation at seeing a woman pleading before the tribunals. Such a want of modesty appeared to the Republic to forebode some calamity, and the Senate sent to consult the Oracle. We have already seen how our Revolutionists imitated the Athenians; we here see in what they reresemble Romans.

But how shall we comprehend, why men—who might have some beneficial influence on our destiny,—who pretend to wish for the legitimate monarchy,—reject Religion?

What, has not impiety yet done enough of evil? Has not enough of blood been shed? Are not Revolutionists yet satiated with proscriptions, spoliations and crimes? Alas! No; we are again returned to sophistry, the sneers and the injustice of 1789. The Priests after the massacre* at the Carmelites—the banishment to Guyana,—the fusillades of Lyons,—the drownings of Nantes—after the murder of the King, of the Queen, of Madame Elizabeth, and of the young King,—the priests, stripped of every thing, without bread, without shelter, are still in the eyes of our enlightened statesmen nothing but *Calotins*†. Well, if it be so, I do not fear to predict that the wish of Mr. Philosopher Diderot ‡ will yet be accomplished.

* In 1793. Tr.

† A nick-name by which Voltaire and the Atheists designated the Clergy. Tr.

‡ I presume M. de Chateaubriand, alludes to the famous wish of "seeing the last King strangled by a rope made of the "bowels of the last Priest." I had forgotten that this was Diderot's. Tr.

CHAPTER LXXXV.

HATRED OF THE PARTY AGAINST THE CHAMBER OF DEPUTIES.

WHEN any event either political or religious counteracts the system of *Revolutionary interests*, and has the consequent tendency of supporting the legitimate family, the party shudders, revolts, thunders, explodes :—Hence the fury against the Chamber of Deputies.

Is it not pleasant to hear our *Constitutionalists* denying the existence of Representative Government,—maintaining that the Chamber of Deputies ought to be reduced to passive obedience—restraining the liberty of the press—puffing the police, and, in a word, completely changing their language, and shifting their characters!

Those who formerly professed the same principles as they do now, were called poor creatures, slaves, enemies of light and knowledge. Are then our Philosophers converted? No, *liberalism*, like jacobinism, for which it is but another name, is always the same. Constitutional doctrines produced the present Chamber of Deputies: but that Chamber having alike supported liberty and religion, the Constitution and the legitimate King, the Revolutionists, furious at this result of twenty-five years rebellion, would have no more to do with the Chamber; they therefore began to declaim against the Representative Government, because they were obstructed by its vigilance, and against the liberty of the press, because they can no longer employ it to their advantage;—free nevertheless to resume their liberal principles, when the royal dynasty shall be changed, and there shall be no danger of the re-establishment of the Altars of God.

It must be confessed that the Chamber of Deputies has done two things which cannot fail to excite the horror and detestation of all true partizans of *Revolutionary interests. By banishing the Regicides*, and suspending the sale of national domains, it has stopped the course of the Revolution: can it ever be forgiven?

Accordingly what efforts have there not been made, first to calumniate, and afterwards to destroy, it! Though elected by the fullest assemblage of the Electoral Colleges, though chosen from among the principal landed proprietors of France, have not foreigners been told that nobody attended these Colleges at the election, and that the Chamber is composed of emigrants destitute of property? If instead of these fanatical deputies who hearken only to the name of their God and their King. France had elected enlightened and practicable Revolutionists, all would have been well—submissive to the rod of authority, these worthies would have offered no resistance to the wishes of the Ministers until the day, when—every thing being arranged—they should think fit to declare in the name of the Sovereign People, that the People wished to change its master!

A thousand projects were formed to get rid of the Chamber: sometimes it was proposed to dissolve it, but no law had been yet passed to guide the new election law: sometimes they thought of dismissing a fifth, but then how was the selection to be made; and besides, what was to be gained by this partial change?

At last passion went so far as to dream of the indefinite adjournment of the Chambers, the suspension of the Charter, and the continuation of taxes by *Ordonnances*.

We saw in the Official Journal of the Police, a laboured eulogium on a certain Minister in a foreign state, who has deferred, until a more convenient time, the promised Constitution; who, by the Royal authority *alone*, governs with admirable moderation, scrupulously discharges the debts of the state, and is enthusiastically adored by the People. Do you not understand? France, I say, do you not understand? You were not used to be so dull—

> Shall all these hints—prepared with so much art,
> Die on the ear and never reach the heart?

A Chamber of good Jacobins, who should be called *Moderates*—or no Chambers at all—such are the wishes of the party. In either case all that it wishes for will be accomplished; *with Moderates* of this description every thing may be destroyed; and *without* them, they will do equally well with a Ministry of their own selection, and *Ordonnances* of their own dictation; and these *Liberals*, who aim at arbitrary power, would soon impute their own arbitrary measures as a crime against the Crown.

I shudder while I unfold a plan so well arranged, and the success of which is infallible; at least, if remedies are not speedily applied. Who would not feel uneasiness at seeing an army so well organised—so well trained—which mines and countermines, and makes use of all sorts of weapons; which enrolls the ambitious and seduces the weak, and which, under colour of independence, preaches up absolute power? And yet it is a faction, cunning and active indeed, but without real talents; a faction, weak and cowardly, easily crushed, and which would hide itself in the earth at a single word; but which, when it shall have enervated and corrupted all, when it is no longer in danger, will suddenly raise its head, and tearing off its crown of faded lilies, substitute for that legitimate diadem the red cap of Democracy or Usurpation.

But, it will be asked, how can you suppose, merely because he may differ from you in a point of politics, that such or such a man—so well known and esteemed for his loyal sentiments, his generous sacrifices, his moral and religious character,—would enter into a conspiracy against the Bourbons.?

This objection may appear formidable to those who do not observe closely, and who judge by externals; yet the answer is not difficult.

One of these persons may have, I admit, served the King all his life: but he is ambitious; he has no fortune, he wants places, he observes that a certain party is the path to favour, and he embraces that party. . . . . . .

Another was irreproachable until the *hundred days*; but during that fatal period he was guilty of mean compliances, and since that has become irreconcilable. He punishes us for the fault which he committed, and the more venomously because this fault shews alike want of judgment and weakness of character;

great personal interests are in fact less inimical to the Bourbons, than little personal vanities.

A fourth, during the *hundred days*, was heroic, but since then his pride has been wounded, and a private pique has induced him to enlist under the banners which he had formerly opposed.

Another is religious, but he has been persuaded that to urge AT PRESENT the interests of the Church, would be highly imprudent, and that too much precipitation might ruin its interests.

Another is attached to legitimate monarchy, but happens to abhor the nobility, and does not much like the priests.

Another loves the Bourbons, has served them, and would serve them again; but he wishes for freedom and the political results of the Revolution, and has strangely taken it into his head that the Royalists are undermining liberty, and wish to undo all that has been done.

Another would be inclined to think that there were some danger, were he not convinced that we are alarmists who only cry out because we are discontented, and because we have been defeated in our intrigues and private plans of ambition.

Others, in fine, and they form the greater number, are careless, frivolous, or pusillanimous, and wish only for pleasure and ease;

they dread the very thoughts of any thing that looks like independence, and take the line of *submission*, weakly fancying it to be that of *quiet*.

I am far from saying that all these persons betray the legitimate Monarchy; but they are the instruments of the faction which betrays it: seeing that they support bad men and revolutionary opinions, the multitude, who do not reason, conclude in favour of these opinions and these men. Thus they mislead by the authority of their example, and thin the ranks of the loyal. When the events shall at last rouse them—when surprized by the explosion, they shall perceive that they have been the dupes of the wretches whom they now protect; that they have served as a footstool to usurpation—they will then be ready to sacrifice themselves for their duty and die at the feet of the Monarch—but in vain—the monarchy will no longer exist.

CHAPTER LXXXVI.

FOREIGN POLICY OF THE SYSTEM OF REVOLUTIONARY INTERESTS.

How shall I speak of the last prop of *Revolutionary interests?* Who could imagine that Frenchmen—to preserve miserable places, to maintain the principles of the Revolution, and to overthrow legitimacy—would have been induced to appeal to the influence of *foreign* powers, and have menaced those who do not think as they do, with measures of force which, thank Heaven, are not within their power?

But you who assure us, your eyes sparkling with joy, that foreigners are pleased with your systems (which I by no means credit), you, who place your opinions under the protection of the bayonets of Europe; did not you yourselves reproach the Royalists with returning in the baggage of the Allies? Did you not evince the most furious hatred towards the generous Sovereigns who came to deliver France from its infamous oppression? What then is become of those heroic sentiments? You, Frenchmen, you so proud, so alive to honour, now submit to avow that "you are *permitted* to have such or such sentiments"; or, "that you are *ordered* to entertain such or such an opinion:" that "a certain Ambassador absolutely insisted that the measure of the Ministry *should* pass, and that the proposition of the Chambers *should* absolutely be rejected:" and (what must be a mere calumny), that "a French minister spent three hours in consulting, with a foreign envoy, the means of dissolving the Chamber of Deputies.." You even venture triumphantly to declare, that a certain *Ordonnance* was communicated to a diplomatic agent, and *that he approved of it exceedingly?"*—And are these forsooth subjects of exultation to you? Which is most a Frenchman, you who talk to me of *foreigners* when we are discussing the laws of my country, or I who addressed to the Chamber of Peers the words which I now repeat: "It is the French blood "which flows in my veins, which excites, no "doubt, the impatience I feel, when, in order "to influence my vote, I am told of authori- "ties which are not those of my country; I "cannot bear foreign dictation, and if Europe "should insist on forcing even the Charter "upon me, I would go and live at Constanti- "nople."

Thus the faction has placed the Royalists in

this critical situation: should they be inclined to oppose the system of *Revolutionary interests*, we are threatened that Europe will force us to silence; and if our mouths are closed by this threat, the destructive system will proceed without interruption, and we and Europe will lament in common the consequence of the delusion.

But, in spite of every risk and peril, I will not be silent; I will denounce this abominable intrigue of a party which prepares our ruin. I at least will do my duty, and I trust that those degenerate Frenchmen are in fact, acting as foolishly as basely. They know but little of the spirit of the nation. If indeed it were dangerous to hold Royalist opinions, we should see the whole of France, even, if on that account only, profess them; a Frenchman readily embraces danger, in the hope that it leads to glory.

Finally, is it surprising that men who have offered the crown of the Bourbons to whoever would accept of it,—who, according to their own expression, would rather have a *Cossack pike and cap*, than a descendant of Henry IV.—is it surprising that the policy of such men should take the colour of their wishes? How should they comprehend that slavery is not obedience, and that independence, as it is the noblest, so it is the safest course. Execute faithfully your treaties; pay what you owe; give, if necessary, your last shilling, sell your last acre, the whole inheritance of your children, to discharge the debts of the State;—but the rest is your own: you are stripped indeed, but you are free!

Away then with idle terrors: the Sovereigns of Europe are too just, too wise, to interfere in the private affairs of France. They have adopted the noble policy of Burke*: "France," says that great man, "must be gained and "settled by *itself*, and through the medium "of its *own* native dignity and property. It "is not honest, it is not decent, still less is "it politic, for foreign powers themselves to "attempt any thing in this minute, eternal, "local detail, in which they could shew nothing but ignorance, imbecility, confusion, "and oppression."

The Allies have delivered their own countries

* Remarks on the Policy of the Allies with respect to France. October, 1793. Burke's Works, vol. vii. p. 148. Ed. 1803.

The Translator takes the liberty of recalling this admirable Essay to the attention of the Public; those who turn to it will find it full of the noblest views, the justest advice, the most precise prophecies, delivered in the most eloquent language; and, for present practical use, it as *fresh* as if it had been written yesterday.—Trans.

from the yoke of France; they know that nations must enjoy that independence, which may be invaded for a moment, but which they must always end by re-conquering:—*Spoliatis arma supersunt.*

Even when our King had not yet been restored to his people, the Sovereigns of Europe had the generosity to declare, that they would on no account intermeddle in the internal government of France; and shall it be pretended that they *now* wish to interfere?—are we to be told that they are alarmed at these debates which belong of the very nature of Representative Government?—that they are displeased at our discussing the existence of a Court of Accounts and the permanence of the Judges?—that they intend to take up arms because our Deputies wish to restore some of its former splendour to the altar—the altar bathed with the blood of so many victims;—or because they have thought fit to exile the murderers of Louis XVI.?

Is it not an insult to these great Monarchs to represent them as hastening to assist the robber or the regicide, and marching armies to support a staggering tax-gatherer, or a falling Minister?

Europe has not less interest than ourselves in maintaining the cause of religion and legitimate order: she must see with pleasure our zeal against these horrible doctrines which had involved her in our ruin. When our tribunals resounded with blasphemy against God and Kings—Kings, justly alarmed, flew to arms: will they now attack those who endeavour to bring back the people to fear God and honour the King!

Who made war upon Europe, who desolated it, who insulted all Princes, who shook every throne? Was it not the men, the very men, whom the Royalists now oppose? Truly, if Divine Providence shall have ordained that the Princes of the earth are now to embrace and cherish the authors of all their misfortunes; to lend their hands to the overthrow of religion, morality, and justice, of real liberty and legitimate royalty—it must be acknowledged that the French Revolution which we had hoped was passed, is but the prologue of a more dreadful tragedy: if Christianity be in danger, it cannot be denied, that Europe is thereby menaced with a general convulsion. Great changes in the political order always attend great alterations in the religious system of states: so true it is that religion is the real foundation of Empires!

Towards you, men of honour, who follow the *Revolutionary interests* by a kind of fatality, I have fulfilled my duty; you are warned; you now see where this system leads you;—will you believe me? I scarcely expect it. You will mistake for the passions of an enemy, the candid and sincere affection of a brother. Hereafter perhaps, when it is too late, you will regret your incredulity: you will then know who were and who were not your friends. You now confide in men who flatter your passions, caress your faults, and humour your weakness; in men who mislead you, and slander you, and are the first to laugh behind your backs, at what they call your incapacity. They urge you to commit faults which they profit by. You fancy they serve you with zeal, while in fact they only wish, some for your places, and others for the overthrow of the Throne which you support. Again I warn you that you will not obtain your object by pursuing the system of *Revolutionary interests:* and that when you think you have attained it, a fatal illusion, a political Calenture deceives you: Athamas, the sport of adverse deities, imagined that he saw the port of Ithaca, the temple of Minerva, the fortress and the palace of Ulysses; he fancied that he beheld—amid his faithful subjects, in the ancient house of his fathers—that king so famous for his wisdom, and his suffering! who in exile and adversity, had learnt to know mankind: but the cloud by which he had been enveloped and deceived, vanished, and Athamas saw nothing but an unknown land, inhabited by a people harrassed by factions, at war with their neighbours, and governed by a foreign king the object of all the wrath of heaven.

CHAPTER LXXXVII.

ARE THERE ANY MEANS OF RESTORING TRANQUILLITY TO FRANCE?

It would be too discouraging, too melancholy, to conclude here. My work moreover would be incomplete.

I have exposed without disguise the dangers with which we are threatened; I have endeavoured to awake those who sleep on the brink of an abyss; I entertain great and well founded fears—but I am not without hopes, which balance those apprehensions; the evil is great, but it is not irremediable, and the remedy, if applied, is infallible.

I have never published any thing without hesitation and self-mistrust; for the first time in my life I now venture to use different language; I venture to make a proposition to restore tranquillity to France.

My plan has doubtless occurred to the minds of many others: it is very simple: but it has not hitherto, to my knowledge, been stated or developed by any one. Prejudices, passions, or interests may perhaps prevent it from being at present adopted; but I do not hesitate to say that it must be tried, or France must perish.

I proceed to explain my proposition—it is no Utopia. With respect to Government, practical things alone are requisite or useful.

CHAPTER LXXXVIII.

GENERAL PRINCIPLES WHICH HAVE BEEN DEPARTED FROM.

SOCIETY in its earlier stages may have been formed by a congregation of men, uniting their interests and passions; but it has been polished and improved only in proportion as these interests and passions have gradually been regulated by RELIGION, MORALITY, and JUSTICE.

No revolution has ever been terminated, but by a recurrence to these three fundamental principles of all human society.

No political change has ever been consolidated and established, but by being founded on the state of things which it replaced.

When the Kings were expelled from Rome, nothing else was changed; above all, the Gods remained in the Capitol.

When Charles II. re-ascended the throne of his ancestors, religion recovered its strength, its riches, and its splendour. Some criminals were punished, some weak men removed. The Parliament preserved the political rights which it had acquired: all things else resumed their course, and proceeded in the old way.

This is what we have not chosen to do; and the legitimate monarchy is consequently threatened with new misfortunes.

CHAPTER LXXXIX.

A SYSTEM TO BE SUBSTITUTED FOR THAT OF REVOLUTIONARY INTERESTS.

According to the principles which I have just laid down, France can be saved only by preserving and maintaining the political results of the Revolution, which have been consecrated by the Charter—putting, at the same time, a final stop to the Revolution itself—distinguishing it from its consequences, and I will say, destroying *it*, that its *consequences* may be secure.

The interests and recollections of old and new France should be as much as possible mingled together, instead of being separated or sacrificed to *Revolutionary interests.*

The Church and the State should be allied for their mutual dignity and safety.

Hence, I am for the *whole* charter—perfect freedom—all the institutions which have grown up by the course of time, the change of manners, and the progress of the human mind—but with them I would preserve all the remains of the ancient monarchy—religion—the eternal principles of morality and justice—and above all I would *not* preserve those men, too well known by their crimes and our misfortunes.

What a paradox it is to pretend to give a people institutions, generous, noble, polished, independent, and to imagine that we can only establish such institutions by confiding them to men who are neither generous, nor noble, nor polished, nor independent: to dream that we can form a present without a past—plant a tree without roots, a society without religion! It is an indictment against the proceedings of all free people: it is disavowing the unanimous concord of all nations: it is despising the opinion of the greatest moralists and statesmen of ancient and of modern times.

My scheme has at least the advantage of being consistent with the rules of common sense, and in accord with the experience of ages.—The execution of it is easy: it is worth the trial.—What have we gained by keeping in the ruts, in which we have been jolting for the three last years? Let us try to get out of them—we have already broken the state coach once—unless we try a new road we shall not reach our journey's end.

CHAPTER XC.

DEVELOPEMENT OF THE SYSTEM:—HOW THE CLERGY OUGHT TO BE EMPLOYED ON THE RESTORATION.

WHEN Dogobert rebuilt St. Dennis he threw into the foundation of the temple his most precious jewels; let us deposit religion and justice in the foundation of our edifice.

All the propositions of the Chamber of Deputies, relative to the Clergy, were not only just and moral, but were eminently politic. Superficial minds did not see this: but what do they see?

Are you desirous that our new institutions be loved and respected? teach the Clergy sincerely to love and respect these institutions.—Let them accompany the King to the ancient altar of Clovis: let them be together anointed with the sacred oil—let there be as it were a joint coronation, and their reign will begin; till then, if I dare so express myself, the Charter will want sanctity in the eyes of the multitude; the liberty which is not derived from heaven will seem the work of the Revolution; and we shall never learn to love the child of our crimes and our misfortunes. What could we hope from a Charter which should be thought endangered by the mention of God and his servants?—from a liberty whose natural allies should be impiety, immorality, and injustice?

But in order to attach the Clergy to your government, remove the proscription under which the government oppresses it—he who distributes the bread of life, should be able to give alms, and not reduced to ask them: associate him to the state, and let not the minister of God be a stranger among men.

Thus, permit the Church to acquire property: restore to it the portion of its land which has not yet been sold.—It is proved by the example of England, that the existence of an endowed Clergy is not incompatible with that of a constitutional Government. To say that if the Church shall possess landed property, the Clergy would become a political body in France, is a chimera which the enemies of religion advance without believing. They know perfectly well how completely our manners and our ideas are now opposed to all invasion on the part of the Clergy.—There are persons—quite as sincere as the others—who are afraid of the Court of Rome!—"Those who, now-a-days, cry *Popery!*" said Dr. Johnson, "would have cried Fire! at "the deluge."

We praise the generosity, the patience, the resignation of the Clergy who ask nothing, who suffer in silence, whilst every body else is complaining and asking for something.—It is edifying to hear us holding forth upon their virtues and letting them, at the same time, die of hunger.

"But to *whom*," it is asked, "are we to restore the property which you would give back to the Clergy? The property did not belong to the Church in general—it was the particular patrimony of monastic orders, of abbeys, of bishoprics, which exist no longer."

How I love to see these pious solicitudes, these truly paternal cares! But still, restore—and let those to whom you make restitution settle their respective rights. It is probable that the Church, which knows how to manage its own affairs, at least as well you, will be able to divide and arrange the little property you can restore to it.

"But the Clergy," you exclaim "will then be organised: they will have a kind of Council"—well; what harm will that do you? Have not towns, parishes, manufactories, councils to manage their affairs!

By this salutary operation, the people will in the first place be relieved from a part of the taxes now levied to pay the Clergy. In proportion as the Church shall acquire property, the assistance which the State is obliged to provide will be diminished.

The Clergy will at the same time resume the dignity which arises from independence,—become landed proprietors, or, at least, drawing an honest livelihood from the possession of the Church—they will be interested in the common prosperity. This act of justice will attach them to government: and you will in them have at your need, auxiliaries alike zealous and powerful.

Increase next their attachment to the new Constitution, by restoring to them, wherever it is possible, the care of keeping of the parish registers.

When a legislator can choose between two institutions, he ought to prefer the more moral to that which is less so. The Christian on coming into the world, receives a name and a faith at the altar of the living God—there is promised to him the means of grace and the hope of glory—there, as it were, he protests against the power of death, and receives a certificate of immortality. The Church, thus receiving him at his first breath, seems to teach that the first duties of man are the duties of Religion, and that these include all the others.

These feelings, so noble and so useful, do not

however, belong to the registers kept for purposes purely civil. They are catalogues of slaves for the law, and of conscripts for Death.

There is no doubt that public education ought to be placed in the hands of Ecclesiastics and religious congregations as soon as possible. It is the anxious wish of France.

The Peerage should be attached to the Sees of all the Archbishoprics: let there be in the Chamber of Peers the bench of Bishops, as exists in the House of Lords in England. I do not see even what should prevent a Clergyman from being elected a member of the Chamber of Deputies. The Charter does not forbid it, if he be a landed proprietor—it would neither offend our manners nor our recollections; for the Clergy formerly constituted the first order of our States General, and we have been accustomed to hear them speak from the pulpit and in political assemblies.

I have no doubt that the Clergy—connected with the soil of France, by the property of the Church,—taking an active part in our civil and political institutions—would at the same time form a class of citizens as devoted to the Charter as ourselves. From the commencement of the Monarchy to the present time, it is incontestible that the first-rate talents have been in the Church: it has furnished our greatest Ministers, as well as our first orators, and our most elegant writers. Into society the Clergy will carry with them a salutary influence, they will heal the wounds of the Revolution, appease the agitations of men's minds, correct morals, re-establish by degrees the principles of order and justice, preach salvation, and finally revive the spirit of religion which is the cement of social life, and of morality, which gives consistence to Political Institutions.

"But will not the spirit of the Clergy be in opposition to the spirit of the Constitutional Government?"

When, I ask in return, was the Christian Religion the enemy of liberty, or of the laws? Has not the Gospel been preached on all the earth? Is it not one of its divine and miraculous characteristics, that it applies itself to all the forms of society.

In the middle ages, Italy was covered with Republics, and Italy was then Catholic, as it is now. Do not the three Swiss Cantons of Uri, Schwitz, and Underwalde, profess the Catholic religion, and have not four centuries elapsed since they set to Europe, then barbarous, the example of freedom? In England, a rich and powerful Clergy is the most assured support of the Throne, as of the Constitution and the time is probably not far distant, when the Catholic Clergy of Ireland will be admitted to the benefits of that admirable Constitution.

In fine, if you leave, as has been done hitherto, the Clergy wholly disregarded, you will necessarily render them hostile, or at least indifferent: a large part of public opinion will follow them and quit you.—The Clergy, poor and wretched, as you will have left them, will be, in spite of you, a wheel within the wheel of the state.—They will more strongly remember the rank they once enjoyed, while you keep them aloof, than when you shall have admitted them to all that you can now impart. If they complain then, it would be without justice, for they must of course feel the modifications that have been experienced by the other orders of the State.

For the rest, when I urge, as the first means of safety, the necessity of the re-uniting the Clergy with the Monarchy, I neither pretend to stop short, nor to go beyond the spirit of the age: I am not unreasonable, and I know very well what can be and what cannot be done. —On this point I expressed my opinion to the Chamber of Peers—let me be permitted to repeat it here:—

" The higher the rank of the peerage," I said, in speaking of the Law of Elections,

" seems to place us above the multitude, the " more zealously we should defend the privi- " leges of the people; let us attach ourselves " strongly to our new institutions, let us be " eager to add to them what is wanting.

" To win to the altar unanimous support, to " justify the rigor we have displayed in the " prosecution of criminals, let us be liberal in " our political sentiments—let us vindicate " every thing that belongs to the independence " and dignity of man.

" When it shall be known that our Religion " is not bigotry—that the justice we demand for " the Clergy is not a secret enmity against phi- " losophy—that we do not wish to see the " human mind retrograde—that we only desire " a useful alliance between morality and talent, " between Religion and the sciences, between " good manners and the fine arts—then no- " thing will be impossible to us; all obstacles " will vanish, and we may hope for the resto- " ration and happiness of France.

" Three pledges, gentlemen, will constitute " our safety; the King, Religion, and Liberty; " it is thus we shall advance with the age and " for ages: and that we shall introduce into " our institutions both what is expedient and " what is permanent."

CHAPTER XCI.

THE NOBILITY OUGHT TO ENTER INTO THE ELEMENTS OF THE RESTORATION.

THE Nobility as well as the Clergy ought to be apart of the constitution, in order to introduce into our new state of society, that tradition of ancient honour, that delicacy of sentiment, that contempt of fortune, that generous spirit, that faith, that fidelity which we so much need, and which are the distinctive virtues of a *gentleman*, and the most necessary ornaments of a state; upon this head I have little left to desire, and the Nobility are naturally, and in right of the Charter, admitted to their places in the new government.

I dwelt at much length in the *Reflexions Politiques* on the subject of the ancient Nobility of France, and upon the advantages they would find in the representative monarchy. I predicted to them that such of the Members as should not at first enter into the Chamber of Peers, would find a noble career open to them in the Chamber of Deputies. I predicted also that they would soon acquire a relish for the present political order of things—Was I wrong? We have seen this or that gentleman, now representatives of the people, who certainly could never have expected to attain that eminence which they reached during the course of the last session. It is the natural result of things—we become attached to what we do—we love that which procures us success.—I ask those who have shone in that Assembly—those whose speeches every man remembers and quotes—those whose talents are respected by France and by Europe—whether the Representative Government *now* appears to them contrary to their real interests? How happy ought they to be to find themselves followed by applause, received in triumph, for having defended at once the King and the People—for having spoken to our unaccustomed ears the language of religion, justice, loyalty, and honour.

Jealousies between the orders of the State—the cause and consequence of the Revolution—will disappear by degrees. What we called formerly noble and *bourgeois*, will soon forget all former distinction in the common title of representative of the people. Proud of so great a trust, and so honourable a name, we shall see between them no other distinction than that which may arise from the diversity of talents and the difference of characters.

I am persuaded therefore that the ancient Nobility of France, who have found in the army new friends and fellow soldiers, enobled by courage and honour;—that Nobility which fills so brilliant a rank in the political system, will soon lose all feeling of regret, and become as firm a support of the Representative Government, as it was formerly of the ancient Monarchy.—Liberty is not new to the French Nobility; they never did acknowledge in our Kings any absolute power but over their hearts and their swords.

CHAPTER XCII.

CONTINUATION OF THE FORMER.—THAT WE MUST ATTACH THE MEN OF FORMER TIMES TO THE NEW MONARCHY.—PANEGYRIC OF THE CONSTITUTIONAL MONARCHY. — CONCLUSION.

SINCE the Restoration, some honest men, dupes of the system of *Revolutionary interests*, have endeavoured to convert the new men to the old feelings. This is exactly the reverse of that which should have been attempted. It is the men of former times whom we would still reconcile to the new institutions.

I admit that our misfortunes may have raised very legitimate prejudices against the Representative Government. But if the ancient *regime cannot* be restored—as I think I have clearly demonstrated in the *Political Reflections*—what would you put in its place?

And besides that ancient government, excellent as it may have been, had it not also, like the actual order of things, its times of crisis and distress. Those who remember the tranquil days which preceded our storms, may believe that such a calm could be produced only by the excellence of the old government; but if we could appeal to our ancestors, who lived during the troubles of the *League*, we should probably not find them quite so well satisfied with the ancient system. The best principles, the most sacred establishments, all human institutions, may be abused. We should have little left if we were to reject every thing which has been the excuse or the result of mortal infirmity.

A Representative Monarchy is not perhaps a perfect system of Government, but it has incontestible advantages. When there is war abroad, or insurrection at home—it becomes, by the suspension of certain laws, a kind of dictatorship. Is a chamber factious?—it is restrained by the other, or dissolved by the king. Should the course of inheritance place on the Throne a Prince hostile to public freedom—the Chambers resist the invasion of tyranny. No other species of Government can impose weightier taxes, or raise greater armies. It is particularlv favourable to arts and literature; under a despotic system, when the Monarch dies! his plans die with him: with Chambers which, continually revived, live for ever, every thing lives, and nothing dies but the individual person of the Monarch; the Chambers resemble in this respect those religious and literary Corporations which never died, and which used to complete immense undertakings which no individual would have courage to attempt, or longevity to finish.

Every man in such a Government finds his use and his place, and the Government, obliged to employ the ablest men, will learn to make use of all ranks and of all ages.

What under the old system of France became of that class of men who had attained "the age "for ripening the fruits which youth had pro-"mised*." What occupations remained for them in the prime of their life and in the fulness of their faculties?—a burden to themselves and others, surviving the passions which animate, and the graces which adorn, youth, they withered in a garrison or at court; in the idle corner of an old country house, or in the as idle bustle of Parisian society;—triflers by profession, endured rather than desired—without any occupation but the gossip of the town, the sittings of the academy, the success of the last new piece; and now and then on great days—the fall of some Minister;—such a life was unworthy the dignity of manhood; and that period of existence, in which a man is fit for any thing, and that in which he is fit for nothing, were employed alike!

Now, the nobler occupations which filled up

* Cic. de Senectute.

the time of a Roman, and which open so large a career in England, will also exist for us; we shall no longer throw away the middle and the end of our days; when we cease to be *boys*, we shall begin to be *men*. We shall console ourselves for the pleasures of our youth, by the solid honours of our maturity. Time will have little effect upon those who see in their duties the road to immortality.

Such are the considerations which should be presented to those honest and virtuous minds, which—disgusted with your ingratitude and your false and Revolutionary principles—view with suspicion our new institutions and sigh after the good old times. Let us hasten to reconcile these men with our present condition: Such efforts have been made to gain over the Revolutionists, that we may hope some will be made to rally round the King and the Charter, the faithful friends of the monarchy.

It is to such men that belongs, as of right, the direction of affairs. Every thing will flourish in their hands, while the others taint whatever they touch. Let men of honour be no longer made dependant on knaves; but employ the good as examples to and checks upon the wicked. Such is the natural order of morality and justice:

Confide to the firm friends of the constitutional monarchy the highest charges of the Constitution. It would not require any immense number to save France; *seven* in each department would suffice; only seven. A Bishop, the Commandant, the Prefect, the * Attorney-General; the President of the Cours Prevotales, the Commander of the Gendarmerie, and the Commander of the National Guard; with these seven men, devoted to God and the King, I would answer for all the rest.

But then we must not have at head-quarters a Ministry, which fetters, restrains, paralyses torments, persecutes, and at last dismisses these seven Royalists, and, on all occasions sacrifices them to mal-contents and conspirators.

Our Ministers must be above suspicion, and distant from all participation in the *morals* of the Revolution; they should persecute nobody, nor permit any one else to persecute; they should be kind, indulgent, tolerant, humane. They should firmly declare that they will permit no *re-action*. They should frankly and affectionately embrace the Charter, and scrupulously respect our rights and liberty.

But they should at the same time distinguish between good men and bad; they should give a preference to virtue over vice; their impar-

* There is one of these officers in each department. Tr.

tiality should not be evinced, by putting an honest man at one desk, and a rogue at the next; they should support boldly and highly our holy faith; they should be devoted to the King and his Family—aye—even to death, if it should be necessary; and *then*, we shall see France arise from her ruins.

As for these able men whose minds the Revolution has debauched,—and those others who would deny to the Throne the support of the altar, the graces of ancient manners, and the reverence of old traditions—let them go cultivate their farms; they may be recalled when their talents, weary of inaction, may have reconciled themselves to God and the King.

As for the herd of subordinate agents, it would be absurd to treat them with equal rigor; place over them proper chiefs, vigilant, and trust-worthy guardians, and you will have nothing to fear from them:—besides, the time for *epuration* is gone by with regard to them.

In the choice of measures, consult the temper and genius of the Nation. Your administration should be economical, but not penurious; it should be, above all firm, vigilant and active.

" Sire," I ventured to say to the King in my Report at Ghent, " it is a wise and useful intention to avoid the excess of activity with which

"Bonaparte harassed the country, but the "French have been for twenty-five years past "accustomed to see the most active government which ever existed;—all was bustle; the "ministers always at work; orders flying "about in all quarters; some new event, some "new expectations for every moment; the "scenes, the actors, and the spectators for "ever changing. Some persons are of opinion that after so much excitation it might "not be proper too suddenly to let down the "springs of action.—It may, say they, afford "too much leisure to discontent; nourish disquiet; and excite injurious comparisons: the "secondary agents, accustomed to be led even "in the most ordinary affairs, will not know "how to walk alone.

"Perhaps in a country so susceptible as "France, and so long plunged in the enchantments of military glory, it might be "expedient to forgive a more than ordinary "impulse to the civil and political Administration.—A more ostentatious attention to "commerce, agriculture, literature and arts;— "great public works designed—great rewards "proposed—a general emulation excited— "brilliant distinctions to successful talents—all "these might tend to give another direction to "the manner and minds of the nation. The cha-

" racter and acquirements of the Monarch, him-
" self a friend to literature and the arts, would
" give them a peculiar splendour;—acknow-
" ledging in their King the soundest judgment,
" the best task, the noblest views, the French
" would enter with ardour a new career—
" and—changing only laurel for laurel and
" glory for glory—the radiant and innocent
" triumphs of peace would obliterate from their
" memories and affections the guilty intoxica-
" tion of anarchy, and the bloody enthusiasm
" of war." . . . .

The sessions of the Chambers should be short but frequent: laws intended to be proposed should be previously meditated. We shall learn in time to condense them as in England; the immense length and innumerable articles of those propositions are a radical defect of our present practice; they lead to everlasting debate and amendments without end.

I shall not pursue further the explanation of my system. I have already traced its leading principles in the preceding chapters of this work. I have still much to say on the subjects of education, literature, and the arts; but I must confine myself at present to great political considerations and hasten to conclude.

A few words of recapitulation. Religion, the base of all well-ordered society,—the Charter—honest men—the political *things* of the Revolution—but not the political *men* of the Revolution—such, in one sentence, is my system. . . .

The precise converse of this system is that which has been adopted—we have been fonder of the men than the things—we have governed according to interest, and not according to principles—we have thought that the masterpiece of a restoration is to keep every body in his place. This barren and timid notion has lost all—for the principal authors of our troubles could not reconcile themselves with a legitimate government; and besides, however clever at pulling down, they had no talent in rebuilding, and the new edifice was therefore without foundation; and the winds of *March* levelled it in the dust.

It is in vain that we put our trust in the good disposition of the army and the Guards—in the composition of the gend'armerie—these to be sure are great points; but they are not enough. The system of *Revolutionary interests*, that political *dry rot* will soon destroy them. It works its way every where, and poisons and destroys whatsoever it touches. Such a system spoils what is good, gangrenes what is bad, and blights the fairest hopes, persecutes the best men, discourages zeal, inflames discontent, and will sooner or later, destroy the legitimate government which is weak enough to foster it.

In the plan which I have proposed, the safety of the monarchy is insured; but I am not ignorant how much courage it requires to execute it. It is easier to attack the patient than the restless; the silent, than the brawler; it is easier to overthrow a Charter which cannot defend itself, than personal interests which are strong and skilful in resistance; but I am not the less persuaded that out of this plan there is no political salvation for us.

Alike mistaken are they who would return to ALL our *ancient* institutions, and those others who advise you to govern France, by the same hands which lacerated her: Fatal error on both sides, France wishes for the *political* and* *material* interests, the rights of liberty and property, which have grown out of the times, and which are henceforward consecrated by the Charter.

But she wishes neither for the principles nor the men that have caused our misfortunes.

This is the whole and simple truth; the Administration which disbelieves it will fall into irreparable error.

My work is done!

I never before wrote with such pain; my pen

* Vide chapter LV. where this is explained.

has often fallen from my hand; and, in moments of discouragement and weakness, I have been tempted to destroy my work. Whatever be its success I shall at least reckon it amongst the good deeds of my life. " *Do what is right and " care not for consequences.*"

I was aware that to alarm my country, which I think in danger; to awaken her before the fire gets head; was a duty which superseded all personal considerations: I have been obliged to tell the whole truth—to offend many men—to jar a crowd of interests. I see, or fancy I see, as I said in my place in the house of Peers, the salvation of my country in the union of ancient manners with modern institutions—of the good sense of our ancestors with the enlightened spirit of this age—of the old glory of Duguesclin with new glory of Moreau—in short in the alliance of religion and morals, with liberty and the Charter.

If all this be a *dream;* the good and the generous will forgive, at least, the wishes which prompted the vision.

POSTSCRIPT.

The Chamber of Deputies is dissolved. I am not surprised; the system of the revolutionary interests goes on. I have nothing to alter in this work. I foresaw the *denouement*, and I have often foretold it. This measure of ministerial vigour will, say they, save the legitimate monarchy. To dissolve the only assembly which, since 1789, has manifested royalist sentiments, is, in my opinion, a strange way of saving the monarchy.

We have seen in the fourth, fifth, and sixth chapters, the constitutional doctrine upon the subject of ORDONNANCES in the representative monarchy. Under the ancient regime, the *ordonnance* of the King was law, and nobody had a right to discuss it. In our new constitution an *ordonnance* is strictly a measure of the Ministers. Every citizen has the right to examine it, and that which is the common right of every citizen is the especial duty of every Peer and every Deputy.

If an *ordonnance* were to bring France into danger, the Chambers might accuse the Ministers. They are the real authors of *ordonnances*, and they may be prosecuted for them.

I am going, therefore, conformably to reason and constitutional principles, to examine without scruple or reserve the *ordonnance* of the 5th of September.

In the first place, it would have been better not to have introduced this *ordonnance* with any preamble.

The King dissolves the Chamber because he has the *right*, because he *chooses* it. Sovereign Lord and Master, he owes to no one an account of his reasons: when he speaks *alone*, every one ought to obey cheerfully, but in profound and respectful silence. We go to a new election, because he commands it: and when he says to his subjects, *I will*, the law itself has spoken.

But the Ministers having stated *their* motives in the preamble, the affair assumes a different aspect; it is our duty to respect—reverence the Royal will: to hesitate a moment in obeying it is a crime. The King can desire only our good—our happiness; but the motives of Ministers are not so clear, and are within the limits of discussion.

Ministers recall to our mind these wise expressions of the King's admirable speech in opening the last session:—" None of us ought " to forget, that close to the advantage of " amelioration is the danger of innovation "

At first it may appear a little singular that

they should have quoted that passage: for upon whom does the reproach of innovation fall? Not upon the Chamber, which innovated nothing—but upon the *ordonnance* of the 13th of July, 1815, which had altered some articles of the Charter. It is a quarrel between *ordonnance* and *ordonnance*, between Ministry and Ministry.

Did not the Ministers, who must have read the King's speech, since they quote a passage of it in the *ordonnance* of the 5th of September, read in that speech the following very remarkable passage?—"Gentlemen, it is to give more "weight to your deliberations, it is to concentrate more light, that I have created new "Peers, and that the number of Deputies has "been increased."

But they had forgotten the speech of the Monarch, as they had before forgotten the acts of their predecessors.

But, in order to refresh their memory, I shall lay before their eyes the preamble of the *ordonnance* of the 13th July, 1815:—

"We have announced, that our intention was "to propose to the Chambers a law for re-"gulating the election of the Deputies of the "Departments. Our project was to modify—"conformably to the lessons of *experience*, and "the *well-known wish of the nation*—several ar-"ticles of the Charter, concerning the con-

" ditions of eligibility, the number of Deputies, " and several other dispositions relative to the " formation of the Chamber, the initiative of " laws, and the mode of its deliberations.

" The misfortunes of the times having in- " terrupted the session of the two Chambers, " we have considered that the number of De- " puties for the Departments is, from different " causes, too small for the full and fair repre- " sentation of the people. It is particularly " important, in such circumstances, that the " national representation should be numerous, " that its powers should emanate more directly " from the Electoral Colleges, and, finally, that " the elections should serve *as the expression of* " *the real opinion of our people.*

" We have therefore determined to dissolve " the Chamber of Deputies, and to convoke " a new one without delay; but as the mode " of election has not been regulated by law, " any more than the modifications to be made " in the Charter, we have thought that it be- " hoves our justice to cause the nation to en- " joy from this moment the advantages which " may be derived from a representation more " numerous and less restricted in the conditions " of eligibility; but wishing, however, that in " no case any modification in the Charter " should be rendered definitive, except accord- " ing to the constitutional forms, the dispo-

" sitions of the present *ordonnance* shall be the
" first object of the deliberation of the Cham-
" bers The whole Legislative Body shall
" regulate the law of elections, and the al-
" terations to be made in the Charter in this
" particular—alterations of which we here as-
" sume only the initiative, on *points* the most
" *indispensable* and *urgent*,—imposing also on
" ourselves the obligation of approaching as
" nearly as may be possible to the Charter and
" to the forms heretofore in use."

Observe, I beseech you, the reasoning of this *ordonnance!*

The Ministers, whose work it is, say—That several articles of the Charter must be modified, conformably to the *lesson of experience and the known will of the nation;* they assure us, that the number of Deputies of Departments has been, from divers causes, *reduced* to a number inadequate to a full and fair representation of the people; they assert that it is of importance that the *national representation should be numerous;* that the elections should serve *as an expression of the opinion of France.* Finally—insisting still upon the same principle—they declare, that though the mode of elections could not be at that time regulated by law, it was nevertheless just to let the nation enjoy forthwith the *advantages she ought to derive* from a *more numerous* representation, less restrained in

All this was true scarcely a year ago—it is false now!

Has, then, the *well-known wish of the nation* changed? The *lesson of experience* and the WELL-KNOWN *wish of the nation* THEN required the *revision* of some articles of the Charter, and NOW Ministers tell us that *the wishes* and *wants* of the French are to preserve the constitutional Charter untouched! At least they ought, for decency sake, to have varied the expression a little.

What must we think, when we see men who had applauded with transport the first ordonnance, applaud with equal violence the second?

We were deceived, then, when we thought the number of Deputies of Departments *too small*. The nation, consisting of 24 millions of inhabitants, will be sufficiently represented, it seems, by 260 Deputies! The departments of the Lozere, and the Upper and Lower Alps, for example, who will have but one Deputy to the Chamber, will they be fully satisfied?

If we change our Ministers every year, are we to have from year to year a new mode of elections? Who can assure me that the Ministers of the next year will not find the representation of this year too numerous? Will not a hundred of their clerks (duly assembled forsooth) appear to them to form a better Chamber, and more in the interests of France?

the Charter;—God grant! it is all I desire; but I am not at all easy upon the subject.

In virtue of the 14th article of the Charter, which gives the King the power of *making rules and ordonnances necessary for the execution of the Laws and the safety of the State*, may not the Ministers see the *safety of the State*, wherever they see the *triumph of their systems?* There are so many *Constitutionalists*, who would now govern by *ordonnances*, that we may see instead of laws, some fine morning, the whole Charter confiscated to the profit of Article xiv.

Let me state the true reason why France is again thrown, as it were, into a lottery wheel.

The party that would drag down France to her ruin would, as the first step, sell the woods of the clergy—it would sell them, not as a good system of finance, but as a good revolutionary measure—not to pay the Allies, but to consecrate the Revolution—and as it well knows that the Chamber of Deputies would never have consented to this sale, it has availed itself of the ill humour and idle terrors of the Ministers, to persuade them, very unluckily, that *their* existence is incompatible with that of the Chamber.

It feared, besides, that the Chamber might, as was its duty, enlighten the King as to the real opinion of France.

In fine, I have already said it, that party has never forgiven the Deputies for having unmasked its projects, and deposed, in the regicides, the princes of the Revolution.

You will read in the papers long and laboured articles in praise of the dissolution of the Chamber, but recollect, while you read, that the press is *not free*—that it is in the hands of Ministers—that it is these very Ministers that have dissolved the Chamber, and written, or paid for, the articles. You observe that the funds rose; but you should know that on the day the *ordonnance* was published, a speculation, a trick was played on the Exchange; and a jobber had the audacity to exclaim, "the *scoundrels shall never return.*" These *scoundrels* were the Deputies!

What are the wishes of the King? If it were permitted to penetrate into the secrets of his royal wisdom, might we not presume, that by leaving constitutionally full liberty of action and opinion to his *responsible* Ministers, he carried his views much further than they? Perhaps he thinks that France may send him back the same Deputies, with whom they were both so justly satisfied—that we shall have a new Chamber as royalist as the last, though convoked upon other principles, and—if that should be the case—that there would then be no possibility of mistake as to the *real opinion* of France.

THE END.

ed its projects, and deposed, in the regicides, the princes of the Revolution.

You will read in the papers long and laboured articles in praise of the dissolution of the Chamber, but recollect, while you read, that the press is *not free*—that it is in the hands of Ministers—that it is these very Ministers that have dissolved the Chamber, and written, or paid for, the articles. You observe that the funds rose; but you should know that on the day the *ordonnance* was published, a speculation, a trick was played on the Exchange; and a jobber had the audacity to exclaim, "the *scoundrels shall never return.*" These *scoundrels* were the Deputies!

What are the wishes of the King? If it were permitted to penetrate into the secrets of his royal wisdom, might we not presume, that by leaving constitutionally full liberty of action and opinion to his *responsible* Ministers, he carried his views much further than they? Perhaps he thinks that France may send him back the same Deputies, with whom they were both so justly satisfied—that we shall have a new Chamber as royalist as the last, though convoked upon other principles, and—if that should be the case—that there would then be no possibility of mistake as to the *real opinion* of France.

THE END.

Lightning Source UK Ltd.
Milton Keynes UK
UKOW05f0632141116
287594UK00008B/67/P

9 781331 338932